W9-AQT-428

Lutheran Theological Southern Seminary   Columbia, S. C.

SUBSTANCE-ABUSING
HIGH ACHIEVERS

LIBRARY OF SUBSTANCE ABUSE AND ADDICTION TREATMENT

A Series of Books Edited By
Jerome David Levin, Ph.D.

Substance abuse and addiction are the third most common cause of mortality in the United States. They are among the most prevalent mental illnesses, not only in the United States, but throughout the world. They are also notoriously difficult to treat. Mental health professionals see few patients whose lives or illnesses have not been profoundly affected by their own use or that of their families or peers. Addiction is not peripheral but central to the human condition and research into it is illuminating our understanding of self.

The *Library of Substance Abuse and Addiction Treatment* is dedicated to providing mental health professionals with the tools they need to treat these scourges—tools ranging from scientific knowledge to clinical technique. Non-ideological, it is equally open to behavioral, cognitive, disease model, psychodynamic, and least harm perspectives. An overdetermined disorder affecting millions of people requires multiple viewpoints if it is to be successfully treated. The *Library* provides those multiple perspectives for clinicians, students, and laypeople as articulated by the most insightful workers in the field. Practical, utilitarian, scholarly, and state-of-the-art, these books are addressed to all who wish to deepen their understanding of and increase their clinical efficacy in treating addiction.

Primer for Treating Substance Abusers
Jerome D. Levin

Treatment of Alcoholism and Other Addictions: *A Self-Psychology Approach*
Jerome D. Levin

Recovery from Alcoholism:
Beyond Your Wildest Dreams
Jerome D. Levin

Couple and Family Therapy of Addiction
Jerome D. Levin

The Dynamics and Treatment of Alcoholism: *Essential Papers*
Jerome D. Levin and Ronna Weiss, Editors

Gender and Addictions:
Men and Women in Treatment
S. Lala Ashenberg Straussner
and Elizabeth Zelvin, Editors

Psychodynamics of Drug Dependence
Jack D. Blaine and
Demetrios A. Julius, Editors

The Hidden Dimension:
Psychodynamics in Compulsive Drug Use
Leon Wurmser

Substance Abusing High Achievers:
Addiction as an Equal Opportunity Destroyer
Abraham J. Twerski

Creating the Capacity for Attachment:
Treating Addictions and the Alienated Self
Karen B. Walant

Psychotherapy of Cocaine Addiction:
Entering the Interpersonal World of the Cocaine Addict
David Mark and Jeffrey Faude

Drug Dependence:
The Disturbances in Personality Functioning that Create the Need for Drugs
Henry Krystal and Herbert A. Raskin

SUBSTANCE-ABUSING
HIGH ACHIEVERS

ADDICTION AS AN
EQUAL OPPORTUNITY DESTROYER

Abraham J. Twerski, M.D.

JASON ARONSON INC.
Northvale, New Jersey
London

Farm Amag ¹²/₁₀ 39.95

The author gratefully acknowledges permission from Oxford University Press to reprint Appendix C from *Alcoholism in the Professions* by LeClair Bissell and Paul W. Haberman. Copyright © 1984 by Oxford University Press.

This book was set in 12 pt. Granjon by Alpha Graphics of Pittsfield, New Hampshire and printed and bound by Book-mart Press, Inc. of North Bergen, New Jersey.

Copyright © 1998 by Abraham J. Twerski, M.D.

10 9 8 7 6 5 4 3 2 1

All rights reserved. No part of this book may be used or reproduced in any manner whatsoever without written permission from Jason Aronson Inc. except in the case of brief quotations in reviews for inclusion in a magazine, newspaper, or broadcast.

Library of Congress Cataloging-in-Publication Data
Twerski, Abraham J.
    Substance-abusing high achievers : addiction as an equal
opportunity destroyer / Abraham J. Twerski.
      p. cm.—(Library of substance abuse and addiction
treatment)
    Includes bibliographical references and index.
    ISBN 0-7657-0110-3 (alk. paper)
    1. Successful people—Substance use. 2. Substance abuse—
Treatment. I. Title. II. Series.
RC564.5.S83T94   1998
362.29—dc21   97-23008

Printed in the United States of America on acid-free paper. Jason Aronson Inc. offers books and cassettes. For information and catalog write to Jason Aronson Inc., 230 Livingston Street, Northvale, New Jersey 07647-1731. Or visit our website: http://www.aronson.com

Contents

Foreword

"I can't be addicted because . . . I'm a doctor! I'm a lawyer! I made over $100,000 last year! I run a Fortune 500 company!"

These rationalizations for addiction have cost the lives and productivity of many thousands of highly successful men and women. This mistaken belief, "I can't be addicted because I'm successful," rests in the myth that addicts are poor, homeless, and/or irresponsible people. Nothing could be further from the truth. Many addicts are rich, living in the best of neighborhoods and juggling massive responsibilities. It is their success that often creates the biggest obstacle to their recovery. Unfortunately, many die from their alcoholism surrounded by family, under the care of the best physicians, in one of the nation's most expensive hospitals. The problem is that they are dead!

Successful people often believe that success makes them immune from addiction. It does not. Addiction to alcohol and other drugs does not discriminate by income level or tax bracket. It does not distinguish a success from a failure. In fact, the pressures of dealing with success and the responsibilities that come with it can, when coupled with the right genetics, increase the risk of addiction. Even though many successful people believe they are different from "other people," when it comes to addiction they are not.

Dr. Twerski calls this problem *terminal uniqueness*. In *Substance-Abusing High Achievers*, he exposes the dangers of such thinking with a simplicity that borders on brilliance. Using actual examples from his lifetime of work in counseling alcoholics, Dr. Twerski presents the complexity of addiction in a way that successful people can readily identify with. He manages to break down complex issues in the addictive process into language that is clear and easy to absorb. The case examples work. I have shared several with some highly successful people in recovery. Their response has been the same—"I wish I could have read this years ago. I never knew other successful people had this problem."

Substance-Abusing High Achievers can be used as a therapeutic tool by counselors. It can also be a means for families to intervene in the abusive drinking of their successful family member. A "Hey, Dad, listen to this" followed by reading one of the stories can effectively confront an alcoholic in a non-judgmental way. After the story is read, simply asking, "Did you ever know anyone like this, Dad?" could set the stage for an important and perhaps lifesaving conversation.

This is an important book for anyone working with chemically dependent people. It is a vital tool for counseling highly successful people who are addicted.

Terence T. Gorski

1

An Equal Opportunity Destroyer

Rich man, poor man, beggar man, thief,
Doctor, lawyer, . . .

Remember that little childhood ditty? I don't quite recall how
it was put to use, but in working with chemical dependency problems, it can serve as a statement of the truly non-discriminatory
nature of addictions. Regardless of who one is, what one is, how
much one knows, or how much one owns, there is always a vulnerability to addiction. No one is immune.

We owe a debt of gratitude to those people who have shed their
anonymity and have shared their histories of alcoholism or other
chemical dependency with us. Former First Lady Betty Ford, Senator Harold Hughes, Elizabeth Taylor, Governor Ann Richards, and
Jason Robards are some of the prominent people who have coura-
geously disclosed their struggle with chemicals and their recover-
ies. Suzanne Somers has called attention to the ordeals and emotional
turmoil experienced by family members of chemically dependent
people. In contrast to those who recovered, we have also been made
aware of prominent people who did not recover, such as Judy

Garland, who fell victim to alcohol; the basketball star Len Bias, whose sudden death from cocaine came only one day after signing a multi-million dollar contract; the multi-talented John Belushi, who lost his life to heroin and cocaine; and Elvis Presley, the singing idol whose career was truncated by a variety of pain pills, tranquilizers, sedatives, and amphetamines.

Some people may nevertheless have greater difficulty coming to terms with their addiction because they consider themselves unique. Some may have a delusion of immunity, whereas others may have great anxiety that acknowledging their problem and especially accepting help for it may expose the condition and jeopardize their livelihood. Thus, although addiction is an equal opportunity destroyer, there is reason for directing attention to those people who may have a greater degree of resistance to diagnosis and treatment.

Denial is the hallmark of addiction. While an individual may deny having tuberculosis or cancer, the denial is not a component of the disease per se. In addiction, however, there is reason to believe that not only does the chemically dependent person deny the addiction, but that the addiction actually *produces* denial. Thus, denial is invariably present in all addiction, at least in its earlier phases.

The basic denial that is indigenous to addiction as a whole can be magnified many times, especially by certain situational factors. Much of the denial consists of the delusion of control, with the individual obstinately insisting that he is really in control of the alcohol or cocaine and of his life in general. The issue of control is extremely important in development of addiction and may be one of the reasons for the apparent increase in various types of addiction in our time.

Before the era of mechanization and electronics, there were not too many things that were subject to human control. For example, prior to the invention of the automobile, travel was by horse and buggy. If the driver wished to turn right, he would pull on the right rein, causing the animal to turn right. While this invariably occurred, the driver did not actually control the horse's action. Rather, by pulling on the rein, he caused the horse to feel a discomfort at the bit and in order to eliminate the discomfort, the horse turned right. Essentially, the driver made the animal an offer it could not refuse. Theoretically, if the horse were starved and there was a pile of hay to the left, it is conceivable that the discomfort of the hunger might outweigh the discomfort of the bit, and the horse would have turned left instead of right.

This changed with the automobile, where the driver does not merely influence the car's behavior, but has absolute control of the direction of its travel. When the driver turns the steering wheel he controls the car in a different way than the driver of the horse and buggy. In this common, everyday phenomenon, people now exert control in a way they had never done before.

I recall as a child, having a little toy truck that I operated by pushing. Today I see little children sitting in one corner of the room, gleefully playing with a little vehicle that is running around at the far corner but is being controlled by a remote control panel in the child's hands. The modern child thus experiences a degree of control that was unknown to me.

When the Explorer II satellite went beyond the limits of the solar system, and beyond the planet Pluto some two billion miles distant from Earth, it nevertheless responded to commands issued from the Space Center. Think of it! Modern man can control objects billion of miles distant.

Our lives are replete with instances of control. We no longer throw wood or coal into the potbellied stove, but rather move a dial whereby we control the temperature in our homes to our desire. We may leave for work with a casserole in the oven, and by a timing device control when the oven will go on or off in our absence. As an alternative we may dial our phone number and activate the oven or any other appliance. We have VCRs that are voice-sensitive, that will not only record programs as we verbally instruct them to, but will also eliminate commercials if we say the magic word "zap." Biologic sciences are forever extending their borders, and with genetic manipulation now a reality we have unprecedented and undreamt of controls.

Modern man may thus find it more difficult to accept that there are things beyond his control, especially when it involves some aspect of his behavior. Such acceptance may be particularly difficult for people in authoritative positions, such as judges, executives, doctors, or lawyers, or others who may successfully exert a great deal of control in their professions or occupations; therefore the idea that they cannot control the use of a chemical is simply unthinkable.

For example, a baseball pitcher who had a phenomenal fast ball and who could control exactly where he wished to place the ball at 100 miles per hour found it extremely difficult to accept that there was an aspect of his behavior that he could not control. (See Chapter 20.)

There are many similarities among these people, and also significant differences. In the pages ahead, I will delineate some of these features, facilitate recognition of the addiction by lowering the resistance thereto, and also encourage acceptance of help by diminishing the anxiety that is so often experienced.

2

The Executive Suite

Alcoholism generally does not begin with daily drinking or intoxication. Very often the onset may resemble normal social drinking, but the drinking then progresses surreptitiously, eventually resulting in harmful consequences. The individual may be able to function at his daily duties for a long time while the disease progresses. Early detection may be possible if dependency is detected, that is, the individual finds it difficult to function normally without a drink.

Case 1: Bill

Bill was a 42-year-old man who had been hospitalized for a recurrent peptic ulcer. His wife, a nurse, was concerned that his drinking was preventing the healing of the ulcer and requested a consultation with me.

When I broached the subject with Bill, he laughed. "Doctor, me an alcoholic? You must be kidding. I will admit that when we go to our cabin for weekends and I'm completely free of responsibility, I may drink heavily. That may happen three or four times a year, but that's deliberate, calculated heavy drinking, not alcoholism."

I asked Bill what his consumption of alcohol was like other than on those weekends and he said, "Some days I don't drink at all, and some days I may have one or two drinks. Except for those weekends, I never drink heavily and when I don't drink, I don't miss it at all. I'll tell you this, doctor. I'm a vice president of the bank, and I'm in charge of twenty-seven banks whose managers are answerable to me. Every Wednesday we meet with those managers, and I do take a double before that meeting to loosen up, because otherwise I'm uptight. But I may not drink at all for the rest of the week."

I said, "You do have an alcohol problem, Bill. There are various types of alcoholism, and one of them is when any normal function has become dependent on alcohol, whether it is eating, sleeping, sexual relations, socializing, or work. By definition, a *normal* function is a necessary one, and if a normal function has become dependent on alcohol and cannot be performed without the addition of alcohol, the alcoholic process has already begun. It is only a matter of time before the body accommodates to that amount of alcohol, so that the double no longer provides the desired effect. Your only options then are either to eliminate the normal function or to increase the amount of alcohol to achieve the desired effect.

For you, conducting a weekly meeting of twenty-seven bank managers is a normal function. If this has become dependent on alcohol, you have already started on the road to full-blown alcoholism. You can either get help to stop now or wait until you are further along the course." We parted very amicably.

Several months later I received a call early one Monday morning. "Doctor, this is Bill. I've had one of my weekends and I feel very shaky. This hasn't happened to me before. I must get down to the office, but I can't go in shaking like this. Is there anything you can give me?"

I replied, "I don't want to add a dependency on pills to the alcohol problem."

"All I need is to get over the shakes today," Bill said.

Rather unwisely, I called in a prescription for six tablets of a non-addictive medication.

Six months later on another Monday morning, there was a repeat performance. "You're going to have to come into the hospital for detoxification," I said.

"Can I be out by Wednesday morning?" Bill asked.

"I doubt that," I said.

"I can't do it, doctor. I have my weekly bank managers' meeting on Wednesday and I can't miss that."

After a good bit of pleading, I yielded, but only after Bill promised that immediately following the Wednesday meeting he would come to my office. When he arrived I said, "Look, Bill, I know something you don't. I know you're on a course that will inevitably result in a crisis. If I keep on bailing you out, the disease process will continue and the crisis will be delayed until you are perhaps 55, at which time recovery will be much more difficult. If the crisis occurs now when you're 43, your recovery will be much easier. I don't want to get any calls from you unless they're for treatment. Under no circumstances will I prescribe any medication to get you over the shakes. If the reaction to your drinking is severe enough to get you into trouble on the job, it's just as well that this happens—the sooner the better. I'm not extricating you from this anymore."

Eight months later I received a call from Bill's wife that he had been hospitalized after driving his car into a telephone pole. He had managed to escape without serious injury and was released from the hospital after overnight observation. He was still unwilling to accept treatment for alcoholism. Somehow he had avoided being charged with drunk driving.

I did not see Bill until three years later, when I noticed him in the audience at one of my lectures on alcoholism. He looked healthy and smiled at me. I was truly pleased to see him. I took the opportunity of including in the lecture a description of dependence on alcohol due to anxiety when conducting meetings or speaking to groups. Several weeks later I received the following letter:

Dear Doctor,

I was just delighted to see you again, and it was very rewarding to see the joy in your eyes. I'm not sure whether your initial facial expression was lack of recognition or disbelief. Whatever . . . it was one of those experiences where words are not needed to describe feelings; the eyes say it all.

I've thought quite a bit about your lecture and your closing remarks. We both know many drinkers who would pay little attention to the consequences you spoke about. I believe that with most people it's an illusion of immunity and not a real "don't care" attitude. After the lecture, you must at times wonder "What good did it do?" In your profession, I imagine it would be easy to fall into the trap of measuring disappointments, because one can't always measure the effects on those who succeed.

I left there knowing I had an additional reinforcement to stay away from liquor. Periodically, I get the old desire, and what has worked thus far is to be able to weigh all the benefits of sobriety vs the pleasure (??) of drinking. I need all the reinforcement available, otherwise denial and rationalization always surface. Although my sobriety is only a little over six months old, it has been and is a comfortable one. I'm aware that it's easy to become complacent, and for me the defense is going to a lot of meetings. Eight or nine a week is average and while there isn't a great need to go to so many meetings, for me it is educational, enjoyable, and gives me the opportunity to better know the people in AA.

Since our first meeting four years ago my drinking has been strictly periodic. But prior to that as I learned recently, I was a daily drinker and a periodic drunk. This makes acceptance difficult, because one hears so many in AA comment that they lost control every time they drank; how could I be a drunk when it only happened four or five times a year? If you ever encounter another person with this pattern perhaps my story may help.

Getting back to the events after my hospitalization, the pattern was erratic, but as you know, predictable. I would be sober for two or three months or even longer, drink for a week, two, or three, taper off and quit. After talking to you from the hospital after the accident, I was ok for six months—drank for two weeks, then back again—quit for a month, then back for another detox last December. Although I knew then I'd lost the battle with booze, it took three more two-week binges to get it out of my system.

During the period from December 1974, to April of this year, I went to AA meetings pretty regularly and became acquainted with Clyde. He arranged for me to go to Alina Lodge, where I spent fourteen weeks. Someday I'll tell you about this experience.

The firm, particularly my supervisor, was very understanding and gave me the time with pay. For this, I'll always be grateful. My supervisor and two of my fellow workers found it difficult to believe I was alcoholic. For a long time, I thought they were being kind, but I recently discovered they were really surprised to learn of my problem.

Most of my drinking in the past four years happened when on vacation, making it easier for me to hide it. In retrospect, I imagine my co-workers could look back and remember situations that were not quite normal. As you can see, I've been very fortunate. However, all of the "I never" could quickly be reversed with an ounce of alcohol. I have only a couple of minor regrets for continuing to drink in the past few years, because it gave me the proof needed to feel the way I do now. Fortunately the body is a great mechanism, and despite the abuse mine seems to be in pretty fair shape.

This was longer than I intended, but writing it was good for me. Thanks for your help and interest.

For executives concerned about subordinates who may have a chemical dependency problem, or for the chemically dependent executive concerned about taking time off for treatment and the reactions of peers who may learn about his alcoholism, the following narrative may be of help.

Jack is a retired executive with fifteen years of sobriety. He volunteers a great deal of time and effort to the operation of a facility for addiction treatment, bringing his much-needed experience as an executive to the administration. He also devotes time to helping newcomers to recovery. Like Bill, Jack was able to continue functioning while his drinking increased. Let us listen to his account.

Case 2: Jekyll and Hyde

"I started drinking in college, and continued in the army, particularly in the year in the service after the war was over. Drinking slowed when I started with the corporation, but increased as I progressed to the position of vice-president in charge of purchasing, with all the free drinks and entertainment that were the perks of that position. After nineteen years in purchasing, I became VP of sales, and later VP and assistant general manager of engineering and construction. This position offered opportunity and freedom for drinking both at home and on sales trips.

"My wife (and others) said I had a 'Jekyll and Hyde' personality, and my too patient and understanding boss said that I would return from a week's sales trip and raise hell with the engineering people with whom I generally behaved well. I'm sure he knew that my problem was alcohol, but he never mentioned it. Instead, he instructed me to see the company's EAP (employee assistance program) counselor. I didn't admit I had a serious problem with alcohol and I returned to work knowing in my heart that I had better watch myself, and I did for two months. I did not read the ten-item questionnaire to see if I had an alcohol problem, because I was both ashamed and afraid to know.

"Just one year later my boss again insisted that I see the counselor, but this time I walked into his office and said, 'I guess I have a drinking problem.' He recommended that I enter Gateway Rehabilitation Center and I accepted his advice. Strangely enough, after telling my family and my boss that very day, I had a tremendous feeling of relief and I sensed that I had reached a turning point. I believe I owe my life to my boss for handling the situation the way he did.

"While I was at Gateway, my boss and some of the staff visited me. He pointed out that only they, the vice president in charge of personnel, and the chairman of the board were aware of where I had gone and why, and that no one else would learn of it. We agreed that for the first ninety days after my return to work, my out-of-town travel would be greatly reduced in order to allow me to make the recommended ninety meetings in ninety days. In my therapy group at Gateway, we discussed possible difficulties I might expect on returning to home, work, and friends.

"On returning to work I found that very few people asked where I had been. If they were close friends I easily admitted that I had been to an alcoholism rehabilitation center, and to others I said I had been 'away for awhile.' I found that people are generally considerate and don't pry. I was cautiously proud of what I had started to accomplish, but I had learned not to boast about it. Most friends, noticing that I did not drink anymore were either pleased or awed, but in any case happy for me and my family. I think that a few might even have been jealous.

"In my relationships to friends or while attending various functions, I found that most people were more concerned with their own lives and hardly noticed that I no longer drank. I think that if they did notice they were happy that I wasn't preaching to them about it. It was a simple thing to substitute coffee, iced tea, or coke, and I did not feel awkward at parties.

"During my first year of sobriety, our family had no parties. There was no sense in tempting the devil. My wife had started going to Al-Anon while I was at Gateway and came to appreciate and learn from it as I had with AA. Her participation in Al-Anon was a help and support to both of us and to our daughters.

"With the help of experienced people in AA, I was able to attend parties at business conventions without succumbing to alcohol. I learned how to entertain customers with little or no temptation to drink. The customers and friends had just as much fun, and there was certainly more responsible behavior on my part. Little wonder that my sales performance improved, since I was now thinking about our customers instead of myself. We lost no real friends due to my abstinence and after a few years of sobriety I was respected more and even envied by a few. On business trips to other cities I attend meetings and have found many new friends in the AA fellowship all over the world. Traveling has become a joy it had never been previously.

"The concerns we had while at the treatment center about reentering the world of business, family, friends, and dealing with challenges and losses were legitimate at the time, but like most things, anticipated troubles are rarely as big as one expects them to be. As my self-esteem increased along with my self-confidence, I learned to handle virtually all situations and personalities much more efficiently."

This case demonstrates the anxiety that many feel about the detection of their drinking problem, their accepting treatment, and their concern about how they will be received when they return to work. It also shows that these feelings are really groundless, and that addressing the problem effectively provides unexpected relief.

3

Surreptitious Development of Chemical Dependency

Addiction to narcotics is not necessarily the result of wanting to get "high." It is no less devastating when potent medications are used quite innocently to treat a condition for which they are medically prescribed. Who would think that taking medication to suppress an annoying cough could threaten a person's career? Gary never thought this could happen.

Case 3: It Was Only a Cough

Gary was a bright young man who breezed his way through high school, getting A's and a few B's with hardly cracking a book. He had decided on a medical career early in life, for two uncles were doctors and they were his heroes. Their lifestyles appeared to be much more interesting than his father's, whose job as a manufacturer's rep lacked pizazz. Gary also liked his uncles' sports cars and knew that as a doctor he could afford one.

College and even medical school were no sweat, although the latter did require some extra effort. Nevertheless, there was enough time for partying. Gary got drunk a few times and used marijuana with some regularity but this never resulted in any problem. In his first year of surgical training, Gary married Barbara who later quit her nursing position when she became pregnant. Within three years they had two lovely children. Barbara was not pleased with Gary's drinking but never took it too seriously.

Gary joined a group of two other physicians in his surgical specialty and within two years his life was going pretty much as planned. He earned well, got his sports car, and Barbara went back to full-time nursing. She was not often around when he drank. No problem. He had launched himself on a very promising career.

But he developed a stubborn cough that just seemed to linger, and neither antihistamines nor antibiotics were of any help. In the kind of surgery Gary was doing, there was no leeway for even the slightest hand tremor due to his cough, and in order to be able to function Gary wrote himself a prescription for Hycodan, a narcotic-containing cough medication.

After several weeks, he was still coughing with the regular dose of Hycodan, but a little larger dose brought the cough under control. This pattern continued, so that Gary was eventually taking fairly large self-prescribed doses of Hycodan. Once the pharmacist said, "Hey, doc, you're sure using a hell of a lot of this stuff," and Gary became concerned that the pharmacist might think he was an addict, using the medication to get high. He therefore went to another drug store for his next prescription and eventually to six other drug stores, so that no single pharmacist would think he was using excessive dosages. He did try to reduce his dosage, but each time he tried the cough became more violent.

What Gary did not realize was that the Drug Enforcement Agency was collating his prescriptions and they stuck out like a sore thumb. Two narcotics agents were dispatched to his office with a warrant for his arrest, since prescribing narcotics for one-self without accurate documentation violates narcotics regulations. Gary explained the problem to his partners and although sympathetic, they informed him that they could not risk the publicity of one of their group being arrested for a narcotic violation. They gave him two months' salary and sent him on his way.

Gary pleaded guilty (there was no option), and was given a $5,000 fine and four years probation. His narcotic prescribing privileges were revoked. He was unable to function as a physician for three years and was then hired by a hospital as a salaried employee. Although he has now been clean and sober for eight years, he is earning less than one-third of what he would have been earning had he remained in his specialty practice.

Gary is an addict. No, he did not get his drugs from a pusher in order to get high, but from a legitimate pharmacy to control a cough that was preventing him from performing delicate surgical procedures. But once you are into addiction, it makes no difference how you got there. You may get to Chicago from the east, west, north, or south, and by car, bus, plane, or hitchhiking, but once you are in Chicago you are there. The same is true of addiction.

Why didn't Gary realize earlier that he was becoming addicted to a narcotic? Because part of the disease process of addiction alters thought processes so that one does not realize that addiction is occurring. This is called *denial* and is quite different from lying, a process of saying something one knows to be untrue. Denial is self-deception, probably an unconscious mechanism, whereby the person denies to himself that he is addicted. At some point Gary's denial broke down and he realized that he was addicted and tried to wean himself off the medication, but his efforts to do so precipitated withdrawal symptoms, especially an aggravation of the cough, which he had to subdue in order to operate.

Why didn't he simply say to his partners, "Look, I have this terrible cough, and I need some time off to get it treated properly"? Because at this point Gary's thinking was distorted by his addiction, and good logic is not a component of addictive thinking.

Why did Gary progressively increase the amount of Hycodan he consumed? Because of the phenomenon of *tolerance*. Tolerance occurs frequently with narcotics, alcohol, sedatives, and stimulants, and simply means that after a period of use of any of these, the body becomes so accustomed to the substance that it no longer has the same effect. It is as though the body has become immune to that amount of chemical. A person who uses alcohol for relief of tension may find that he needs ever-increasing quantities of it to relieve the tension. The person who uses pain pills may find that she is no longer relieved by the same dose, and an insomniac may remain wide awake after he takes his usual sleeping pill. When the chemical stops working, the person who depended on it for relief of tension, pain, or insomnia, will do what appears to be sensible: take more.

Although Gary's cough might have cleared after a period of time, the fact that he became addicted resulted in the cough becoming a withdrawal symptom, so that even if the reason the cough occurred in the first place was gone, the cough now continued as the body's signal that it needed more Hycodan. The body's craving for narcotics can have various manifestations. The heroin addict who does not get his usual dose begins to experience cramping, cold sweats, muscle pains, and diarrhea. When the addiction occurs as a result of pain treatment, the major withdrawal symptom is pain. If it is a result of treatment of a cough, recurring cough is likely to be the major symptom. It is as though the body knows what it must do to obtain the drug.

Would Gary's use of Hycodan have resulted in addiction if he had not had a history of alcohol and marijuana abuse? There is no way of knowing. Certainly a person with a history of alcohol dependency is much more vulnerable to becoming addicted to another drug, but it is possible for addiction to cough medication, pain pills, or sedatives to be the first symptom of addiction. Couldn't Gary's partners have noticed something was wrong and intervened earlier? They probably had no awareness of his addiction. Gary functioned perfectly normally even while he was taking large amounts of medication. Addiction may not impair a person's functioning for many years.

Had Gary not been a physician, he would not have had easy access to this narcotic medication. He might not have bought drugs on the street and likely would have sought medical help, in which case the physician would not have prescribed so much medication. The relatively easy access to drugs makes medical personnel more susceptible to drug abuse.

4

Some Facts about Addiction

We have seen people with great intellectual capacities achieve marvelous feats, both in science and in the arts. They can make momentous decisions, sometimes affecting an entire nation. They may be able to organize numerous details, process a myriad of data, and come to a firm conclusion which they may implement with authority and precision. Is it possible then that such great thinkers cannot restrain themselves from drinking when it is so obvious that alcohol is blatantly destructive? Why is it that their will power, which is so efficient in everything else they do, fails them in regard to alcohol?

Case 4: When the Mighty Fall

Roger was voted "Most Likely to Succeed" by his class. One classmate wrote in Roger's yearbook that he would one day be president and would take the oath of office saying "So help me Roger," because he thought he was God. Roger graduated summa cum laude and in law school became law review editor. He was hired by a prestigious law firm, but after two years left because he was often in sharp disagreement with everyone else there.

Roger had drunk quite a bit during college and law school. He married Nancy, his childhood sweetheart, who strongly disapproved of his drinking, but he dismissed her comments. He was arrested for drunk driving had an altercation with the arresting officer, but managed to get the charges dismissed. He was involved in a brawl at one of the pubs adjacent to the courthouse and was reprimanded for conduct unbecoming an attorney.

Roger's wife gave birth to twins and he celebrated so intensely that he did not show up to take her home from the hospital, and she was brought home by her father. The family chastised him for this, but he said they just didn't understand his need to celebrate the happy occasion with some friends (at 11 am), and this could have happened to anyone.

When the children were 2, Nancy developed some strange physical symptoms and was diagnosed with multiple sclerosis. Roger loved her deeply and this was an overwhelming blow. Nancy had a fulminating variety of the disease and died after five years of progressive deterioration. During this time Roger felt very sorry for himself and his drinking increased. His peers understood his distress and offered to help in whatever way possible.

Roger had neglected the cases of several clients and complaints were filed against him with the disciplinary board. Four registered letters from the disciplinary board went unanswered. Several friends pleaded with him to at least respond to these letters, but Roger stated that if the disciplinary board were crass enough to take action against him in his situation of having lost his wife and trying to care for the children while carrying on an active law practice to support them, he would take the disciplinary board before the circuit court.

The disciplinary board was apparently not intimidated and Roger's license to practice law was suspended. He felt victimized and continued to drink. The children whom he had tried to care for were taken by the grandparents and Roger continued to drink to assuage the injustice resulting from the disciplinary board's insensitivity to his plight.

He did recover, but of that later.

You might ask, why couldn't a person of such intelligence exert his willpower and avoid destructive drinking? The answer is that alcoholism is a disease not amenable to willpower.

When chemical dependencies or addictions are referred to as diseases, many challenge this term, contending that lifting a glass to one's lips or injecting a psychoactive substance is an entirely volitional act, and should not be grouped with conditions such as pneumonia, diabetes, or cancer. Other critics contend that addictions are simply moral or characterological weaknesses, resulting from failure to exercise one's willpower. They may also add that labeling addictions as diseases is nothing but a whitewash, releasing an individual from responsibility from his or her errant behavior.

In 1956 the American Medical Association recognized alcoholism as a disease, a chronic, progressive disease with complications sometimes culminating in death. Since then, several studies have added support to the disease concept.

Whereas it has long been known that children of alcoholics have a much greater likelihood of becoming alcoholics than children of non-alcoholics (a ratio of 4:1), this could easily be understood as a learned behavior. However, repeated studies have conclusively demonstrated that children of alcoholic parents who were adopted by non-alcoholic foster parents and never exposed to the behavior of their biological parents, still had the same 4:1 ratio of becoming alcoholic. Other studies of identical twins who were raised in separate foster homes also revealed that if one twin became alcoholic, the chances of the other twin becoming alcoholic were very great.

These findings leave no doubt that there is a genetic factor in at least some varieties of alcoholism.

Another significant discovery was that of the T.H.I.Q. phenomenon (Tetrahydroisoquinolone). T.H.I.Q. is a substance frequently found at autopsy in the brain of heroin addicts, but it has also been found in the brain tissue of some alcoholics who had never used heroin. It is an abnormal metabolic product resulting from a combination of acetaldehyde, an intermediate product in the breakdown of alcohol, with dopamine, one of the neurotransmitters in the brain. Experiments with monkeys, who usually shun alcohol and favor water instead, have demonstrated that when T.H.I.Q. is introduced into their brains, they avoid water and take to alcohol. Therefore, we have at least one model where the compulsion for alcohol is biochemically mediated. Although this particular phenomenon may exist in only a small number of alcoholics, it does show that there may be a metabolic basis for some cases of alcoholism. Continued research in this field is certain to reveal additional biochemical routes.

Let me confront a possible objection at this point. There are those who argue that the disease concept releases the addict from assuming full responsibility for his or her behavior. This is incorrect. An individual must always be held responsible for his behavior. Concepts such as "temporary insanity" and "irresistible impulse" are not legitimate defenses. Because of a reputation of advocacy for treatment of alcoholism and other addictions, I am frequently called by defense attorneys to provide testimony on behalf of their clients who are charged with drunk driving or commission of a crime while under the influence of alcohol. When I tell these attorneys that in such cases my testimony will favor the plaintiff, that is the last I hear from them.

Many people drink judiciously and are not adversely affected by alcohol. Others have an unusual emotional reaction, or lose control of their consumption, or develop a dependency on alcohol. These abnormal reactions that occur only in some people may be seen as analogous to food allergies, where some people can eat strawberries with no untoward effect while others react with a skin rash or hives, and if the hives unfortunately happen to affect the epiglottis, they may die from eating a single strawberry.

The difference between an allergy to strawberries and an abnormal reaction to alcohol is that the pathological effect of the strawberry is on the skin, leaving the brain unaffected and hence capable of making the causal connection that eating strawberries results in hives. The primary pathologic effect of alcohol in the sensitive person is not on the skin, but rather on the brain, which is responsible for analysis and judgment. Affected by alcohol, the brain cannot make the causal connection, and any untoward effect of alcohol is attributed to every other possible cause, however remote and absurd. This is what I meant when I said that alcohol may produce denial. Recovering alcoholics say that alcoholism is the only disease that tells you that you don't have the disease.

In a culture that promotes and encourages consumption of alcohol by seductive advertisements on billboards and in magazines and by happy hours and cocktail hours prior to banquets, one can hardly be faulted for taking the first drink. As already mentioned, the abnormal reaction that occurs in the alcoholic is not detected by the drinker, and when others point it out, the same pathologic cause results in denial of the problem. Just as you cannot be faulted for taking the first drink, you can hardly be faulted for not recognizing the often insidious progression of the disease. Most often the intensity of the denial progresses concomitantly with the progression of the disease and is not overcome until some crisis or "rock bottom" phenomenon results in a breakthrough.

Roger did reach "rock bottom" and recover, but we will return to that.

Another addiction equally or even more severe than alcoholism is prescription drugs. People who complain to their physician about pain, insomnia, anxiety, or persistent cough are often prescribed painkillers, sedatives, tranquilizers, or cough medications, all of which may be highly addictive. Serious addiction to these medications can occur, with the person being totally unaware of what is happening. In the addiction-prone person, use of a painkiller may actually intensify the pain as the body builds up a tolerance for the substance.

Whereas we might not be able to fault someone for taking the first drink, or the person in pain, or the insomniac who enters addiction via legitimate prescription, the same cannot be said for those who use marijuana, heroin, cocaine, speed, hallucinogens, or any other illicit drug. These people knowingly took illegal drugs for recreational purposes and became addicted to them.

Granted, they did wrong. However, the *disease* was not in picking up the drug for the first time but in becoming addicted to it. Many people have used marijuana only to set it aside and many others have used any of the other drugs and decided that it was not for them. Why is the addict unable to do this? Why does the initial use of the drug exert such a viselike hold on him that he is unable to put it down? Therein lies the disease component.

But this does not justify drug experimentation. To expose oneself to illicit drugs is foolish, reckless, and a violation of the law, in spite of the fact that many important public figures, including some presidential advisors, have favored legalization of drugs. Experimentation is not excusable and those who discontinued use of drugs after experimenting are no less guilty of a foolish and illegal act than those who continued its use. The point is that the continued use is not the wholly volitional act people assume it to be, and, as with alcohol, there is some abnormality with the addict that makes him or her oblivious to the addiction and makes cessation without assistance virtually impossible.

Another fact that suggests something more than lack of willpower is involved is the phenomenon of cross-addiction. It is frequently found that once a person has become addicted to *any* mood-altering chemical, he or she is highly vulnerable to addiction to any *other* mood-altering chemical. For example, a recovered alcoholic who has never used any other chemical and was abstinent for several years may be given a potent pain medication for a physical disease. Unless the medication is rigidly controlled, there is a high risk that she may develop a dependency on this chemical.

Case 5: Linda

A 31-year-old woman was admitted to the rehab center because of relapse. Eight years earlier she had been treated for alcohol addiction but had maintained total abstinence in the years that followed. At this time she developed a persistent cough which was most annoying and interfered with her work and she consulted a physician. Examination did not reveal any respiratory infection and the doctor told her he could give her something to relieve the cough. She told the doctor that she was a recovering alcoholic and was not permitted to take any potentially addictive medications. The doctor prescribed Hycodan (dihydrocodeinone) saying it was not addictive. Initially she was relieved of her cough by the prescribed dose of one teaspoonful four times daily but after two weeks when it no longer suppressed the cough she increased the dosage. This increase in dosage progressed and the doctor refilled the prescription.

Linda was an executive secretary in a small company and although she had always been extremely efficient, she began having difficulty remembering things. Her employer confronted her with these lapses, whereupon she broke into tears, told him of her past history, and that she felt she had now become addicted to cough medication. He was quite unsympathetic to her problem and promptly dismissed her.

Cross-addiction can occur across all lines and in all directions—among alcohol, stimulants, narcotics, sedatives, tranquilizers, and euphoriants. It appears that the brain of the addicted individual is highly vulnerable to habituation to all these chemicals.

Let us move now to the compulsive component of chemical addiction. Yielding to a compulsion is not necessarily a totally voluntary act. However, compulsivity cannot be used as a mitigating factor to relieve a person from full responsibility for her behavior, since this would make every criminal act excusable. But purely from a psychological perspective, some compulsions may be so intense that they require a degree of control beyond many people's capacity. An example of this is post-hypnotic suggestion. A person under hypnosis given a suggestion to perform a certain act after emerging from the trance may be virtually powerless to resist.

A medical student on his psychiatry rotation expressed an interest in hypnosis and asked to be hypnotized in order to experience hypnotic phenomena. I complied with his request and was able to demonstrate various hypnotic phenomena to him. I then decided it would also be helpful to demonstrate a post-hypnotic suggestion, and I told him that after he emerged from the trance I would stroke my beard, whereupon he would rise and place his chair on my desk. I also told him that he would have no memory that I had told him to do so.

After he emerged from the trance, we continued to discuss various hypnotic experiences and I nonchalantly stroked my beard. After a few moments the student became visibly agitated.

"There is something strange going on," he said. "I have the urge to pick up my chair and put it on your desk."

"Why would you want to do that?" I asked.

"I don't know. It's just a nutty feeling I have. Did you tell me anything like that when I was in the trance?" he asked.

"Yes, I did," I responded.

"Oh, well that explains it. But how come I don't remember your telling me this?" he asked.

"Because I told you that you would not remember the suggestion," I said. "That is the nature of a post-hypnotic suggestion."

"Then I don't have to do it, do I?" he asked.

"I guess not," I said.

We finished the session and the student left the room. About twenty minutes later the door flew open and a very angry student burst in, seized the chair, and slammed it on the desk. "Damn you, anyway," he said.

Compulsions that occur in obsessive-compulsive disorders are not the purely psychological phenomena they were long considered to be. These neuroses may respond rapidly to medications, especially anti-depressant medications, although they are generally quite resistant to intensive psychotherapy. Obviously, some chemical in the brain must mediate these compulsions and when this chemical is neutralized by specific medication, the compulsive neurosis essentially disappears.

Compulsions can come in various sizes and shapes and one cannot generalize about them. The point here is that it is possible for the compulsion to use mood-altering chemicals to be so abnormally intense as to warrant classification as a disease. While this does not in any way excuse an individual's behavior, it does justify a treatment approach.

These various features of addiction should explain why the condition can affect a college professor as well as a grade-school dropout and a wealthy executive as well as a street person. Certainly there are both social and individual personality factors that can either facilitate or inhibit the occurrence and development of addiction, but the vulnerability should be understood to be truly non-discriminatory.

5

The Negative Self-Image

A rather constant finding among chemically dependent people is a negative self-image that antedated the use of chemicals, usually by many years.

Negative self-image refers to a self-assessment as inadequate or unworthy that is not in keeping with the facts. In other words, there are people who are oblivious to their personality assets and true worth and see themselves as being much less than they are. In his book, *Alcoholism: The Tragedy of Abundance* (1982) Phillip Hansen says that without exception alcoholics are gifted people. He adds that if there is an alcoholic in any mixed group of people, that person will be as gifted, or more gifted, than any of the others. Over 150 years ago, Abraham Lincoln addressed the Washington Temperance Society, and is reported to have said, "If we take habitual drunkards as a class, their heads and their hearts will bear an advantageous comparison with those of any other class. There seems even to have been a proneness in the brilliant and warm-blooded to fall into this vice. The demon of intemperance even seems to have delighted in sucking the blood of genius and generosity."

Case 6: Margaret

Margaret was admitted for treatment of alcoholism following a suicide attempt with barbiturates that resulted in a three-day coma. She was a 37-year-old board-certified specialist who had lost a prestigious position due to alcoholism.

At age 17, Margaret had been anorexic. Her grandfather suggested that she could gain weight if she drank beer, which is rich in calories. Margaret discovered that in addition to providing calories, beer made the world an easier place to live in. She continued to drink through her college years, eventually switching to spirits when the quantity of beer necessary to provide her need for alcohol became too great.

By the time she assumed directorship of a medical facility, Margaret was consuming copious quantities of alcohol and was then confronted by the dilemma of what to do about the morning "shakes." She could not function while she was tremulous, yet the odor of alcohol on her breath at 8 am was not appropriate for a medical director. She then noted that vanilla extract had thirty-five percent alcohol content and did not have a telltale odor, so she began her day with a stiff dose of vanilla, supplementing it with sips during the day as necessary. At home she switched to vodka.

During her treatment it was apparent that Margaret was a superior person, excelling in many areas. Yet, she had no concept of her excellence but to the contrary was mired in profound feelings of inferiority. When I asked her to describe some of her personality strengths, she remained silent. I pointed out to her that there was undeniable evidence attesting to her excellence. She had graduated summa cum laude and had won the Phi Beta Kappa Award. "When I asked you to list your personality strengths, the least you could have done is to acknowledge your intellectual superiority. They don't give Phi Beta Kappa awards to imbeciles," I said.

Margaret sighed. "When they told me I had won the Phi Beta Kappa Award, I just knew they had made a mistake."

Underestimation of oneself is extremely common and is a major factor in many maladjustments. A distorted self-concept, by definition, is a distortion of reality: the person is in fact gifted and deserving, yet sees herself as being inadequate and unworthy. Proper adaptation to life cannot be made when one's perception of reality is distorted.

Insofar as addiction is concerned, a negative self-image can be a contributing factor in two ways. First, there appears to be an inherent resistance to ruining an object of beauty and value. An awareness of one's true value would militate against doing things that are self-ruinous. Second, recourse to mind-altering chemicals is often an escape from stressful situations and challenges. A person who thinks himself capable is likely to cope with the normal stresses and challenges of life, although a person with a negative self-assessment may see these as overwhelming, opt to escape rather than to cope, and may resort to chemicals as an escape.

If one listens carefully to recovering people describe their early lives, one often hears reference to feelings of negativity present in childhood. One physician, after thirty years of sobriety, reflected about his early years. "I did not take my first drink until I was 17, and I did not start my serious drinking until I was 26. But I can remember when I was 9 feeling that I was different from everybody else, and that everyone else was better than I was."

Many psychological and emotional symptoms are caused by a negative self-image. It is also possible that the negative self-image contributes to an adjustment that may superficially appear most beneficial, but on deeper analysis is fraught with problems.

The proper approach to a negative self-image is to correct the distortion, so that the person can see herself as she is in fact: competent and worthy. In the absence of such correction, a person may attempt to escape from the distress of feeling inferior and inadequate by compensating for fantasied incompetence and unworthiness, and may do so by trying to *prove himself* competent and worthy.

The fallacy in this latter adjustment is that one can never successfully compensate for a deficit that exists nowhere except in one's fantasy. It is possible to compensate for a defect that exists in reality either partially or fully, as for example, the visually impaired person who develops an acute sense of touch or hearing to compensate for the visual loss. Where the defect does not exist in reality, however, compensatory efforts invariably fail because there is no end point. It is like trying to fill a bottomless pit, and this results in enormous expenditure of effort and much frustration.

There is a significant difference between someone who asserts himself because he is ambitious and someone who does so in order to prove himself, although to the observer, these two may appear identical. The ambitious person may be compared with a nursing mother who is uncomfortable until relieved by the infant's nursing. Within several hours she is again uncomfortable because her milk has been replenished and is again relieved by the infant's nursing. Although she is repeatedly giving, it is because she has something to give and is in distress until she does so. Another example is the professor who has a need to impart his vast knowledge to his students. I believe we can all recall instructors who clearly enjoyed giving of themselves to their students. Such assertion of oneself can be considered *ambition*, and although the person may be continually dissatisfied, it is because, like the nursing mother, she now has more to give. This person is nevertheless *satisfied* with what she *has* done, although she has the urge to do more.

The person who has the need to prove himself is operating from a radically different basis. Although he may be very gifted and competent, he does not truly feel that way. He is haunted by feelings of inferiority and in order to prove to others as well as to himself that is he *not* inferior, he tries to excel, and may indeed succeed in excelling. However, his success provides, at the very best, only a brief period of relief, because as already noted, one cannot compensate for a non-existent deficit. This person is promptly driven to do more and this pattern continues. In contrast to the ambitious person, he who has to prove himself has no lasting satisfaction from what he has achieved and is in a constant state of tension and frustration. While such individuals may be great achievers, success comes at a great cost of tension, high blood pressure, coronary artery disease, digestive disorders, migraine headaches, or alcoholism and drug addiction.

Since one of the ways people may cope with unwarranted feelings of inferiority is to try to prove themselves, it is understandable that among successful professionals or business executives we are apt to find many overachievers who are driven to achieve in order to compensate for their feelings of inadequacy.

An interesting finding is that the intensity of an individual's feelings of inferiority is often inversely proportional to her actual qualifications. Thus, if we were to classify people with negative self-images as to their actual positive personality assets on a scale from one to ten, those with a plus three positivity, who are not too well endowed, would have a negative self-image of a minus three magnitude, whereas someone who is in actuality a plus ten, would have a negative self-image of a minus ten magnitude. Since very profound negative self-images may particularly occur in the most gifted people, it follows that if these people are driven to overachievement, they do so with their substantial resources and may therefore be the most successful.

Yet, as already stated, these compensatory mechanisms do little to relieve the unwarranted feelings of inferiority, with the result that in spite of the person's intense efforts of over-achievement, the feelings of insecurity and tension persist. While to the entire world he appears to be a smashing success and a Rock of Gilbraltar, he is really a very frightened person, haunted by the specter of failure and frequently wracked with the emotional and psychosomatic consequences of tension.

I was requested to see a patient with severe peptic ulcer disease in psychiatric consultation. He was a man in his early forties who had been extremely successful in real estate development. He led many important civic and charitable organizations and had received numerous tributes for his community activities. I found him to be a very insecure person who had asserted himself in order to gain recognition. The reassurance he received from public tribute provided only a very transitory relief, because he wanted it to compensate for a nonexisting deficiency. His exact words were, "If you come into my house, doctor, you will find an entire wall of my large living room bedecked with plaques I have received. I look at them, but they mean nothing to me." While the community certainly benefited from this man's efforts, it could have reaped the same benefits had he done so in order to provide for the community's needs rather than to satisfy an insatiable need for affirmation.

His peptic ulcer was not only aggravated by his constant struggle for recognition but also by an appreciable amount of alcohol he consumed to relieve tension. Although he claimed to be following his doctor's order for a bland diet, he did not see that alcohol was a much greater stomach irritant than some of the restricted foods.

While this man seemed to have no peace of mind at all, there are others who do achieve a sense of comfort, but only in their professional or business function. One physician was highly respected by his colleagues, admired by the nursing and house staff, and virtually worshiped by his patients. He would begin his day with hospital rounds at 7 am, leave the hospital for office hours in the afternoon, and return to the hospital in the evening, often remaining until midnight. It was generally assumed by the nurses that his home life must be most distressing, since he never appeared to be in a hurry to go home.

This physician asked me to see his wife for treatment of a depressive episode. She turned out to be a very lovely, sensitive woman, nothing like the shrew the nurses thought her to be. She said, "You know how dedicated my husband is to his work. I am a very insecure person. I needed a shoulder on which to rest my head, but he was never there for that. My children grew up without a father. When they were sick he took excellent care of them, but he was never there to listen to their needs or provide guidance."

I knew this doctor to be not only an excellent clinician, but also a very fine human being, warm, caring, and very personable. However, he had a correct appraisal of only one part of his personality, the professional part. He knew that he was an excellent diagnostician, educator, and therapist, and he felt competent and very comfortable in his role as a doctor. He did not think of himself as having any competence as a *person*, and hence did not feel he had anything to contribute in the role of a husband and father, where his medical acumen was of no value. He therefore felt uneasy at home, because he thought himself to be inadequate as a husband and father, and preferred the hospital and office, where his feelings of confidence made this role a comfortable one. While this doctor had not resorted to drinking, he was a food addict with a very serious obesity problem.

There may be a hidden agenda in the professional life of a person with a negative self-image. As a result of the drive to prove himself, he may need a successful outcome as a vindication. Thus, a doctor may have a need for a patient to recover in order to reaffirm that he is indeed a competent physician. A teacher may have a need for his class to have a sufficient number of high performers in order to reaffirm that he is indeed a competent teacher. When the desired result is not forthcoming, professionals may feel that not only has their inadequacy been confirmed to themselves, but that it is now also evident to others as well. Failures are often triggers (rather than causes) for use of addictive substances and for relapses after some abstinence has been obtained.

If not for the negative self-image and the need to prove oneself, a person might more easily realize that the outcome of any effort is not within one's control alone. A jury may return an adverse verdict in spite of a lawyer's excellence in defending the client, and a patient may have an unfavorable result in spite of the best treatment possible. There are many factors that determine outcome that are not in any way subject to a person's control. The person with a negative self-image, however, has a skewed perspective and is apt to interpret everything in a self-depreciating manner.

In her book, *Famous Women and Alcohol*, Lucy B. Robe (1986) describes "the impostor phenomenon" that often occurs in celebrities and reveals that 40 percent of successful people secretly believe they are fakes or impostors. Paradoxically, in these people successful achievements result in self-doubt rather than self-confidence. Although they consciously fear failure, a fear they keep secret, unconsciously they fear success.

I suspect that this phenomenon is not limited to celebrities, and may occur with equal frequency in other people of stature. For the negative self-image person who is a victim of the impostor phenomenon, successful achievements do not eliminate the sense of inferiority, but ironically, intensify it.

We will be encountering the negative self-image concept numerous times, particularly if we listen carefully to the personal accounts of people who are chemically dependent. In their own way, each alludes to having had a low self-esteem and how this contributed to the addiction.

6

Denial and Rationalization

We generally assume that what we see, hear, and feel is reality. This is not always so. When the brain is affected by a toxic substance, a person may hallucinate, seeing objects that are not there. The reverse may also be true, that we may sometimes not see something that is right before our eyes. This may occur when to perceive reality is too overwhelming, in which case we may have the reverse of a hallucination and be oblivious to reality. This is called denial.

Case 7: When Truth Is Too Painful

A 50-year-old woman was admitted to the hospital for exploratory surgery because of a suspected tumor. She told the doctor that she was very active in community affairs and had assumed many important responsibilities. She realized that a tumor might mean cancer, but it was important for her to know the truth, since it would be unfair to many people and many organizations for her to carry responsibilities if her health and ability to function were going to deteriorate. The doctor promised to be frank and reveal all the findings of surgery.

During surgery it was found she indeed had a cancerous tumor that had to be removed, and, because there was some indication that the tumor had already spread, it was decided to give her a course of chemotherapy. Complying with her request for complete truthfulness the doctor advised her that a malignant tumor had been removed, but there was good reason to believe that with chemotherapy the condition would be arrested. She expressed her gratitude to the doctor for being truthful with her and stated that she would cooperate with whatever treatment was recommended. She spoke freely with the nurses and the staff about realizing that she had cancer.

The administration of chemotherapy required intravenous injection and this particular patient had difficult veins, so multiple attempts were necessary each time the chemotherapy was administered. On one occasion, I was called upon to administer the medication and, as luck would have it, I found a good vein on my first try. The patient then concluded that I had some unusual skill in giving intravenous injections and requested that I administer all of her medication.

Upon discharge from the hospital, she returned weekly for her chemotherapy. She would state that she came in for her "cancer" shot and often remarked how fortunate she was to be living in an era when science had provided a successful treatment for cancer. She appeared to be adjusting well, both physically and emotionally.

Some five or six months after her surgery, she began to have various symptoms; the cancer had spread in spite of the chemotherapy. Eventually she developed severe joint pain and shortness of breath and was admitted to the hospital for further treatment. I did the admission workup on her and she remarked, "I can't understand what is wrong with you doctors. I have been coming here regularly, and you just haven't been able to find out what's wrong with me."

This woman's remark was astonishing to me, since she had repeatedly referred to her having cancer. It then became evident that as long as cancer was some kind of abstract concept to her, which she did not feel was posing an immediate threat to her life, she could accept the diagnosis. Once the condition progressed to the point of causing pain and shortness of breath, and there was concrete evidence that she was deteriorating, this was so threatening to her, that her psychological system shut off the realization of the truth. She was not intentionally lying or pretending. At this time, she actually did not believe that she had cancer.

This, then, is what denial is. Just as a person may faint from sudden severe pain (the body's way of providing relief from perception of the pain), so does the psychological system provide for unconscious rejection of a perception that is too threatening for the person to accept.

Denial is the hallmark of chemical dependency. As the previous example shows, denial is not the same as lying, since lying is a conscious, willful distortion or concealment of fact, while denial refers to an unconscious process. A liar knows he is lying, but a denier does not know he is denying.

This is not to imply that chemically dependent people do not consciously lie. To the contrary, they may be very adept at lying. But much deeper than the lying and much more difficult to deal with is the unconscious denial.

Anyone who has worked or lived with a chemically dependent person can appreciate what denial is all about. The dependence on the chemical and the loss of control are blatant, yet they insist that they can leave it alone or stop any time. The deterioration of work habits is sufficiently severe to elicit numerous reprimands and threats of dismissal, but the chemically dependent person is unable to see that his or her job is in jeopardy. The home may be a shambles and the children alienated or nervous wrecks, but the chemically dependent person makes no connection between this and the drinking or using. Neither convulsions, DTs, drunken driving arrests, nor severe physical illness are attributed to the chemical. No amount of pleading, scolding, or threatening is able to break through the barrier: He insists that he simply does not have an addiction problem.

A pivotal point appears to be the conviction that loss of control of a chemical or of its effects constitutes a personality defect or weakness. For men, particularly, this may stem from a myth that it is manly to drink, that to be able to consume a large quantity of alcohol without showing its effects is indicative of great will and self-mastery, and that the ability to drink everyone under the table is a sign of strength or sophistication.

Having a negative self-image can affect denial, because when loss of control is perceived as a character weakness, the difficulty of accepting powerlessness is generally related to one's true sense of self-esteem. A person who has a fundamental feeling of adequacy and good self-worth is much less threatened by discovery of a limitation. However, the person with a poor or fragile sense of self-worth may perceive powerlessness over alcohol and/or drugs to be a confirmation of his inadequacy, and when the latter is ego-shattering, it must be denied. Thus, denial of chemical dependency is apt to occur primarily in people who have a poor sense of self-worth.

As was mentioned earlier, the pathological use of chemicals may occur when a person turns to them as an escape from the discomfort of normally stressful situations. The only two possible responses to a challenge are either coping with it or escaping from it—the classic "fight or flight" reaction. Escape will be the response of choice when the person feels a lack of strength or capacity to cope. When people encounter a force stronger than they, as when one's car is stalled on a railroad track with a powerful diesel lo-comotive oncoming, escape is indeed appropriate. But when we escape from normal stress into the anesthesia of alcohol or drugs, a pattern of escapism develops, which becomes a part of a person's lifestyle. Escapism can occur in persons who are, in fact, very adequate and capable, but who retreat from coping because they do not *feel* that they are adequate and capable.

Two essential components of addiction, namely escapism and denial, can thus be seen as related to feelings of inadequacy or low self-esteem. The person with the tendency to escapism is prone to denial, and the person with the tendency toward denial is prone to escapism.

Some people may be motivated to become professionals or executives because it gives them a sense of power or control. The many stories about how some doctors think they are God reflect the omnipotent fantasy that may prevail among some doctors. Teachers are people who wield a measure of power and control over their students. Lawyers may experience a sense of power over some aspect of their clients' lives. Executives and administrators exert control over people in various ways. People with a negative self-image are particularly prone to crave power, since this may relieve their feelings of impotence secondary to their fantasied inadequacy and unworthiness.

One recovering lawyer stated, "Even today, after seventeen years of abstinence from alcohol, I still vividly remember the surge of power I would get when I drank. It was a great feeling. I loved it then, and I love it now. The only difference is that now I know that this feeling is only an illusion of power and not the real thing." People who have used cocaine give graphic descriptions of the "Superman" feeling that the drug provides, and it is clear that this was a major component of the drug-induced euphoria for them.

The chemically dependent person thus denies both loss of con-trol and dependency. Actually, dependency is simply another variety of loss of control, since being dependent on a chemical and not being able to function without it is essentially a loss of control. If one *must* have a chemical, then one has lost control of being able to function chemically free.

Although denial is an unconscious process, the awareness of one's dependency on chemicals and the inability to discontinue their use in spite of the overtly harmful consequences frequently threatens to break through into consciousness. The psychological system therefore shores up the denial by means of *rationalization* or giving logical-sounding excuses in place of true reasons. In the case of chemical dependency, the function of rationalization is to justify the drinking as being normal under the circumstances. The most frequent rationalizations take the form of "If you had my ———— (husband, wife, father, mother, children, boss, neighbors) you'd drink/use too."

An executive who conducted his business efficiently but came home drunk every night stated, "When I leave the office, the day has been as good as it's going to get. My home is like a refrigerator. My wife has not communicated with me for the past ten years. Yes, I do stop off and have two beers (actually ten) on my way home. Anyone in my position would do the same thing." This man denied his alcohol dependency, explaining away the drinking as an understandable reaction to a frustrating relationship. It did not occur to him that he had reversed cause and effect, and that his wife was noncommunicative because there was simply no one to communicate with when he returned home in an intoxicated state.

Rationalizations run the gamut from absurd to ingenious. It is obvious that the more resourceful a person is, the more clever his rationalizations may be. Highly intelligent people may have very convincing rationalizations, but unfortunately their brilliance turns against them, since they thereby have greater success in self-deception, hardly a success to be happy about.

A tragi-comic example of denial is related by a physician, a board-certified cardiologist, who drank heavily. His definition of an alcoholic was someone who had to have a drink first thing upon arising. Inasmuch as he never drank until after office hours, he considered himself a social drinker rather than an alcoholic. As time and the drinking progressed, he began to experience "morning-after" distress, but because he had ruled out the possibility of alcoholism, there was no reason to give up drinking. He came to the conclusion that his "morning-after" distress was due to failure of the stomach to absorb the alcohol, with the result that it remained in the stomach overnight and thus caused his early morning discomfort.

This physician had attended medical school during the Great Depression. He was in desperate need of money, and when the medical school offered students five dollars a week (a substantial sum in those days) to be subjects in an experiment, he seized the opportunity. The research involved studying what transpired in the stomach during the digestive processes. The subject would be given specific foods to eat, and forty-five minutes afterward was to insert a tube through the nose into the stomach, aspirate the stomach contents, and submit them to the laboratory for analysis.

Twenty-five years later, this physician remembered that he had become quite skilled in passing the tube into his stomach. Inasmuch as he understood his problem to be due to residual alcohol in his stomach, his brilliant solution was to continue to drink until bedtime, then pass a tube down his nose into the stomach and evacuate the stomach contents. He indeed felt much better in the morning.

"I continued this practice every night for two months," the physician said, "and the only reason I stopped was that the frequent passing of the tube had begun to irritate my throat, and I was in danger of needing a tracheotomy in order to breathe. But never did it occur to me, even once during those two months, that a social drinker does not pump his stomach every night before retiring." This is an example of a highly educated and very bright individual maintaining denial of his alcoholism in spite of blatant evidence to the contrary, with a practice so absurd that every thinking person would consider it grossly abnormal.

Another tragi-comic incident exemplifying denial is related by a prominent attorney with over thirty years of sobriety. In his youth, some senior members of his firm told him that he must get his drinking under control and urged him to join Alcoholics Anonymous. He refused, claiming that being seen at an AA meeting could stigmatize him and jeopardize his career.

Prior to Thanksgiving Day, a committee from a charitable organization for whom he had been doing some work gratis presented him with a gift of a turkey, dressed and wrapped in butcher paper. "I remember leaving the office carrying the turkey. It was a rainy day. The next thing I can remember is coming to at one of the busiest intersections downtown, leaning against the building, holding this turkey under my arm, the rain having washed away the butcher paper. Anyone passing by would have no problem determining my status, as I had exposed my alcoholism for all the world to see. But to walk into a church where there was an AA meeting, why I couldn't do that! Someone might put two and two together and think I was an alcoholic."

Closely related to rationalization, and sharing with it the task of reinforcing denial, is *projection*, whereby a person attributes his own behavioral defects to others. Thus the addict sees others as selfish, inconsiderate, unreliable, and unpredictable, whereas he is free of these negative traits, and is an innocent victim of other people's thoughtlessness.

Rationalization and projection are methods whereby the chemically dependent person justifies the addiction. There is no reason for him to change, because he has no problem. He is merely reacting to the intolerable stress that everyone is placing upon him. Let the others change, and he will have no need for excessive use of chemicals.

Unfortunately, when chemically dependent people seek counseling from mental health professionals who are not familiar with addiction, the rationalizations and projections may be sufficiently convincing that a therapist accepts these as valid, and then becomes an unwitting contributor to persistence of the addiction.

7

The Dependency Problem

On the Fourth of July, we celebrate Independence Day, and in the rituals of the day we pay tribute to our forefathers who achieved the ultimate in human existence: independence. The word itself has charm. It is a concept that appears to embrace the greatest good in life, as though all the positives are included under that rubric. By the same token, *dependence* is a pejorative term, with a connotation of weakness. Little children, the infirm and disabled, the poor, are dependent. Ergo, independence is strong and good; dependence is weak and bad.

However, this is rather inconsistent with the facts of life. In one way or another, we are all dependent. A community consisting wholly of scientists and philosophers would soon perish. We need our butchers and shoemakers and garbage collectors. This dependence on others does not seem to deflate our ego, because we do not expect ourselves to be self-sufficient in every way. However, if we see ourselves dependent in an area where we think we should be independent, that is perceived as a weakness and as demeaning.

Case 8: The Vicious Cycle

Tom and Susan met as freshmen in graduate school and were married before Tom entered law school. Susan obtained a well-paying job and essentially supported Tom through law school. Tom was very bright and joined a prestigious law firm, but his psychological makeup was such that he could not accept the fact that he had been dependent on Susan for his education. Furthermore, Susan would be a living symbol, forever confronting him with the fact that he was indebted to her for his successful career. The original understanding had been that at some point after he had established himself Susan would leave her job, they would have a family, and then switch dependencies. Susan did nothing to provoke Tom, but his background as the child of an alcoholic father was such that he did not see the mutuality of their agreement. Although the facts were that for the remainder of their lives Susan would be dependent on Tom as the provider, this was not enough to overcome Tom's inordinate sensitivity, and his resentment toward Susan took root and grew.

Endowed with a genetic vulnerability to alcoholism and unable to cope with what he perceived as his dependence on Susan, Tom began to drink. As the drinking progressed, Susan began to monitor Tom, watching and controlling his consumption at parties, driving him home, and eventually driving him to the office when his "morning after" coordination was impaired. As is so typical in alcoholism, Tom's dependence on Susan increased exponentially, as did his resentment of his increasing dependence on her. This is a typical example of the vicious cycle of dependency and addiction.

There seems to be a quest for independence that is instinctive rather than rational. Careful observation of small children who lack the capacity to contemplate the abstract concept of independence reveals that they, too, may be fiercely independent. They may fight off parental attempts to help them, insisting on doing things themselves. There is reason to believe that this assertion of independence occurs primarily because they are so totally dependent on adults that they wish to deny it.

When the idea of "I am dependent" is anathema, a person may seek to deny it by the psychological defense mechanism: "I am *not* dependent on others. Others are dependent on *me*." This is translated into action when a person becomes a service provider: doctor, lawyer, teacher, nurse, and so on.

What is wrong with this adaptation? Nothing, if it remains confined to one's occupation, but a great deal can go wrong if it precludes accepting the reality of being dependent on others in various ways.

Dependency may generate resentment. Much of the resentment that is sometimes seen in children toward their parents and the bitter defiance that may occur, may be due to the child's inability to deal with her dependence on her parents as a necessary fact of life. Many of the occupations we have highlighted may serve the purpose of denying one's dependency needs by becoming a service provider.

There is such a thing as "healthy dependence," as, for example, the dependence of small children on their parents, or that of infirm persons on those who help them. A fairly safe rule is that healthy dependence follows when an individual cannot *in reality* do certain things for himself, and is realistically dependent on others. Pathologic dependency exists when one depends on others for things that one *can* do oneself. Of course, like all rules, this one has its exceptions.

Although we will discuss codependence a bit later in greater detail, it might be pointed out here that the rule for codependence is the converse of that for dependence. In other words, doing for others what they can do for themselves is codependence, while doing for them what they cannot in reality do for themselves is healthy, caring consideration.

Dependence is a very complex concept and clinically is fraught with many inconsistencies and contradictions such as Tom's need to deny his dependence on Susan resulting in behavior that led to an ever-increasing dependence on her.

A person may not be able to distinguish between healthy and pathological dependencies and Tom's behavior is a case in point. Since Tom was unable to support himself through law school, his dependence on Susan could be seen as healthy. Assuming Susan did not hold this over his head, there was no need to deny or resent it. Why then did he deny it? Possibly because his self-image was such that he considered any dependency to be a sign of weakness and therefore demeaning. Here we have an example of the complexity of dependence. Tom may have been at least partially motivated to become a lawyer because of his negative self-image, which he felt he could overcome by being in an authoritative position and have others dependent upon him. The very choice of his profession may have come from the need to deny his own dependency needs. He was unable to accept the realistic dependency on Susan, since this generated much discomfort and a confirmation of the dependency needs he wished to disown. The rejection of healthy dependence thus started the development of a pathological dependence.

Healthy dependence is a fact of life and should not be denied, and there is a common sense realization of this in the recovery program. When I was planning the opening of our rehabilitation center, which was to be compatible with AA philosophy, my psychoanalytic mentors were critical of me. "All you will be doing is transferring the patient's dependency from alcohol onto AA." This did not faze me, since my training had not convinced me that psychoanalysis could eliminate dependency needs. A later meeting with a group of people in recovery brought a comment from a thirty-year veteran of sobriety. "We alcoholics are dependent people. When we recover, we transfer our dependency from alcohol onto AA." What the psychoanalysts had seen as a drawback was seen by the AA members as a positive achievement. As a highly functional administrator of a governmental agency, happily married, with a wife, children, and grandchildren who loved him, this man could attest to the value of transferring dependencies and substituting a healthier one for a sick one.

In the complexity of the dependence problem, healthy and unhealthy dependencies become confused, resulting in some of the inconsistencies alluded to earlier. An example of this is the business executive who fiercely asserted his independence several days after a heart attack by detaching his intravenous tubes and signing himself out of the coronary care unit, but had no difficulty in calling his doctor every two weeks for a refill of his pain pills for his low back discomfort. He had become increasingly addicted to these pills and was using them in large amounts, but could not see this as a dependence and refused to consider any treatment. His wife, who became concerned about his drug addiction, sought the help of an addiction family counselor. Her account revealed this man's utter dependence upon her, which he was able to deny. He never bought his own clothes, and every day his wife laid them out for him. She accompanied him on all his business trips, because he was unable to look after his own needs. This total dependency was denied by his grandiosity. "Of course I can do all these things myself, but I am involved in major business transactions of far greater importance, and I don't have time to waste on such trivia as to what to wear with what, or what to order from room service." He was able to successfully deny his total dependence on his wife by exaggerating the importance of his business affairs.

Denial of dependency is not always successful and sometimes things occur that break through the denial. In such instances, the person may be confronted with the actuality of his dependency. The consequences of this may vary but are rarely happy. The shattering of the omnipotent fantasy that had maintained the ego may result in severe depression. In some instances the husband may resent the wife, who, by providing for his excessive demands, is a living symbol of the neediness he is unable to tolerate. He may deny this neediness by rejecting his wife, essentially saying, "It is not true that I am needy and that you provide for all my needs. I am not needy at all and as proof of that, I don't need you!" This is frequently a factor in the failure of marriages, or in a conscious or unconscious demeaning of the wife by involvement in extramarital affairs. In many instances, awareness of one's dependency results in increased recourse to alcohol or other chemicals, seeking the emotional oblivion which can relieve all distress, albeit at an exorbitant cost.

Another variety of dependency is when one depends on others for one's ego needs, that is, for affirmation of one's adequacy and worthiness. Thus, a doctor may become dependent on his patients' expressions of gratitude for their recovery, a teacher may become dependent on his students' demonstrable excellence, and a lawyer may become dependent on favorable verdicts for his clients. The threat of an unfavorable result may impact so heavily on a person that it distorts his judgment, and results in a drive for success at any cost. This may cause the doctor, teacher, or lawyer to engage in desperate maneuvers that may actually be self-defeating. Since outcomes are not under one's control, the suspense while awaiting the outcome can be extremely anxiety provoking, and an ultimate unfavorable result can be ego shattering. Depressions and addictions have been triggered by unfavorable results or treatment failures where the lawyer, teacher, or physician had invested his or her ego as well as a great deal of effort.

Dependency and self-image are intricately interconnected. A person with healthy self-esteem will be able to accept the reality of appropriate dependency and will not be dependent on external factors to vindicate her existence.

8

Honors and Medals

We cannot see in the dark. Yet, although it is light that makes vision possible, sudden expsoure to a bright light, such as exiting from a dark room into the sunlight, can be blinding. If one is blinded by the glare of the sun upon emerging from a dark tunnel, one may not see an oncoming car. Much the same can happen in addiction, when the brightness of one's performance blinds a person to the recognition of what alcohol and drugs are doing to him.

Case 9: From the Heights to Skid Row

Jim was 49 when he was admitted for alcohol detoxification. He was living alone, sleeping in the backs of empty trucks or in doorways, having spent his welfare checks on liquor. The day following admission he left the hospital against medical advice.

Jim was the youngest of three children, and had reason to believe that his coming into existence was a mistake. His father was a ne'er-do-well, and the family lived on the fringe of poverty. Jim swore to himself that he was going to be a success. He was a bright student, getting A's with relatively little study and working at odd jobs to make money. He put himself through college, getting a degree in business administration at 24, and was promptly hired by a major construction firm. Determined to advance, he indeed had a meteoric rise. His innate brightness, diligence, and dedication brought the desired results. He rose rapidly on the corporate ladder, and at age 32 was next to the CEO, a level never previously reached by anyone so young. Jim had married at 27, and he and his wife, Amy, had three beautiful children.

The beer drinking that began at college parties progressively increased, but initially did not affect his work because he drank only at home. He dismissed Amy's disapproval of his drinking as an overreaction, since she had been the child of an alcoholic father. He felt he couldn't be an alcoholic because he only drank beer and never touched the hard stuff. When Amy threatened to leave if Jim did not curtail his drinking, he told her she was being unrealistic, but was at liberty to do as she saw fit. She then took the children and went to live with her parents several hundred miles away.

Jim's drinking continued to progress, and several of his associates told him of their concern. Jim dismissed the possibility of his being an alcoholic as an absurdity. Hadn't he received several awards for outstanding performance at the company? Hadn't he been chosen "Man of the Year" by the Junior Chamber of Commerce? Hadn't he been cited for his leadership of the United Way? Hadn't he been written up in the national journal as a shining example of the economic leadership of the future? Hadn't he been awarded an honorary doctorate by his alma mater? Is that typical of an alcoholic? An alcoholic is someone who is jobless, penniless, and drinks cheap wine immediately after awakening. To insinuate that he was an alcoholic was both insulting and stupid.

But the drinking ultimately led to his dismissal. He still had substantial savings, which he drank away. He would sit in a bar, fantasizing that at any moment one of the head hunters for the

Fortune 500 would approach him with an offer to become CEO, as though these people looked for candidates in bars. Eventually, he drank away his home, his car, and most of his welfare check. Two years later, Jim was readmitted for detoxification. "I know I walked out on you last time," he said, "but I'm ready to do whatever you say."

"Why are you more ready now than two years ago?" I asked.

"You know how much you get for selling your blood, Doc?" Jim asked. "Twelve beers."

"I guess when you sell your blood for beer, you've reached rock bottom," I said.

"Not really," Jim said. "I've been doing that for a year."

"Then what brings you here today?" I asked.

"When I was with the corporation, I was very active in the United Way," Jim replied. "In fact, one year I ran the drive single handedly. This past week I've been panhandling quarters. I can't live that way, Doc."

Jim eventually became the skid row person he had envisioned an alcoholic to be. He had been a full-fledged alcoholic long before that, while he was collecting the laurels and honors bestowed upon him. These achievements had reenforced his denial of his alcoholism. No alcoholic could possibly achieve so much.

This is where Jim was mistaken. Alcoholics do receive honors and awards. They are often overachievers whose enormous drive results in many accomplishments. This occurs at the stage of alcoholism prior to the development of impaired performance. They are elected to high public office, receive Oscars and various sports championship trophies, but they are bona fide alcoholics nonetheless, whose drinking will eventually deprive them of all they had striven to achieve.

The popular concept that an alcoholic is a skid row bum, or at the very best someone who is struggling to keep his head above water, and that an addict is a heroin junkie who alternates between nodding off and stealing VCRs, reenforces the denial of someone who is alcohol- or drug-addicted but is still functioning well. Not only is the addict himself deceived by his successful functioning, but those around him—wife, family, friends, employer, doctor— may also fail to realize the presence of an addiction problem in someone who is operating in high gear.

Case 10: Saint Theodore

Ted and Marilyn came from a city several hundred miles distant, allegedly because they heard of my expertise in drug addiction. Inasmuch as there were several excellent facilities in their own community, I suspected other reasons. The session began with Marilyn describing what an honorable person Ted was. He was quite wealthy, having inherited money and invested wisely. He was a prominent member of the church and was responsible for the church budget. He loved working with young people and had arranged various sports events for children at his own expense, which he refereed or umpired. He sat on the boards of several foundations. He was so highly thought of in the community that when the pastor was on vacation, he conducted the services. Ted sat through this eulogy beaming with pride at this wife's adoration, but I became a bit impatient.

"Look," I said to the wife, "I cannot believe you flew 600 miles just to tell me why your husband should be canonized. How about telling me the grizzly facts about his cocaine use?"

Ted and Marilyn were stunned. "But you don't understand. He's an excellent husband, a devoted father, and highly respected by everyone. We came here because we can't afford to have his reputation tarnished in the community."

She continued: "Ted had his office remodeled and the contractor promised to have it done by a certain date. When the date approached and the work was not finished, Ted told him that he was going to enforce the terms of the contract that specified a completion date, and that he was going to deduct $500 a day for each day beyond the specified date. Two days later the work was nearly complete and Ted was amazed. He asked the workmen how they had done it; they said that they had worked around the clock without sleep and that they were able to do so because they used this drug. They gave Ted some cocaine to try and he liked it."

At this point I had had it with the wife's running interference, and asked, "If Ted has a problem, why isn't he telling me about it himself?"

Ted began by trivializing his cocaine use. He had only been curious initially, but because he suffered from recurring depression and the cocaine had miraculously lifted it, he continued to use it.

I told the couple I would try to help, but only if they stopped playing games. They had come all this way because there was a major problem, and I must know what it is.

What gradually emerged was that Ted had been a regular cocaine user for at least the past year and had left the city several times for a week or two, returning in an indescribable condition, dirty and disheveled. Most recently he had disappeared for two weeks, but had not left town. Rather, he had been in a local crack house and had been with prostitutes. One of them got his identification from his wallet, and recognized his name, and was now threatening to blackmail him. So he was not to be Saint Theodore after all, but to hear his wife's accolades, one would never have guessed.

Robe (1986) describes how public adoration enjoyed by celebrities blinds them to the reality and the severity of their addictions. Furthermore, just as Marilyn was protective of Ted, the collusion of the press, the employer, employees, friends, and even doctors "protect" the celebrities from awareness of their addictions, thus allowing their malignant conditions to progress and take their tragic toll in mental illness, premature death, and suicide.

For all these reasons, people of distinction have greater difficulty in being diagnosed early, if at all, and receiving proper treatment. They are therefore prone to experience greater suffering and more tragic consequences than people of lesser note.

9

The Show Must Go On

Sacrificing oneself for the show to go on places greater importance on the show than on oneself. We thus have two conflicting concepts emerging from "the show must go on." One is the grandiose statement, "The show cannot go on without me. I am of the utmost importance." The second is "The show is far more important than I am," a statement essentially of self-effacement. Such contradictions are not uncommon, especially in chemically dependent people whose lives are replete with conflicts and internal contradictions.

Case 11: The Doctor's Dilemma

Roy was an excellent surgeon, a rising star in his field. Indeed, he had been voted by his class as "most likely to succeed," and had begun to fulfill this prophecy.

But then things began to sputter. Roy was too often unavailable when on call ("My beeper batteries went dead"). His charts were incomplete ("I have more important things to do than fill out silly papers"). He would fall asleep during conferences ("I was up all night with patients"). He failed to show up for a scheduled operation ("The O.R. nurse fouled up the schedule"). All signs pointed to addiction, but there was no evidence. Cynthia, Roy's wife, denied that he drank or used drugs.

Roy was reprimanded several times by the chief of surgery, and each time his behavior improved for several weeks, only to deteriorate again. Then the hospital pharmacist produced a list of drugs that Roy had prescribed for himself. He had become careless and had written prescriptions for himself at the hospital for large amounts of sedatives and analgesics. Roy could no longer deny the problem but refused to enter treatment promptly because he had a busy surgical schedule. He could not afford to take time away from his practice now because people's lives depended on him. When told that he would not be permitted in the O.R. because of his extensive drug use, he protested bitterly. How dare anyone deny others the salvation of his surgical skills! He agreed not to schedule any new cases, and when the currently scheduled operations were finished (he was adamant about that), he would enter treatment. Again he was told that now that his drug use was known he would not be permitted into the O.R. and he broke down and wept.

The slogan, "the show must go on" is not restricted to stage performers. It is a rather common occurrence in individuals who place performance of any kind above life itself. Doctors report cases of executives who signed themselves out of the intensive care unit several days after experiencing a major heart attack. Once the acute pain subsided, they were unable to remain in the hospital because they "had important business that required their presence." This is also characteristic of the alcoholic or drug addict, who after being correctly diagnosed and instructed to enter treatment will say,

"Yes, I will go into treatment, but I cannot do so until negotiations are completed . . . or until there is closure on a multi-million dollar contract . . . or until the case in court is resolved."

It should be obvious that the insistence that one must be present for the show to go on is actually a grandiose assertion. A fact of life is that no one is indispensable, and the world continues to spin on its axis even when some very important people are no longer there or able to function. "It can't go on without me" is a statement made by a person who needs to feel that way. As we have already noted, many people who occupy positions of importance are in those positions precisely because they are overachievers, and the drive to overachieve is a defense against their profound feelings of negativity. It comes as no surprise, then, that the alcoholic or drug-addicted VIP will insist that whereas he may indeed need treatment, it must be deferred until he has completed a task which cannot possibly be brought to fruition without him.

Another aspect of "the show must go on" is the issue of priority. This is addressed by the AA slogan, "First things first," which in AA refers to sobriety. It is axiomatic that anyone who places *anything* ahead of sobriety is likely to relapse. If the show must go on regardless of all other considerations, then "the show" has top priority.

While selfishness is a despicable character trait, there is one variety of selfishness that is commendable. When flying on a jet, the flight attendant gives the following instructions: "In the event of a change in cabin pressure, oxygen masks will appear before you. If you are traveling with a child, put your own mask on first and then attend to the child."

Is it realistic to expect a loving parent to place his own vital needs ahead of the child's? The answer is that if the parent tries to put the child's mask on while he is in a state of oxygen deprivation, the child will not get adequate oxygen nor will the parent. If the parent puts his mask on first, he will be capable of tending to the child's needs and both will do well.

In order to care for your family, your job, or any other obliga-
tion, you must be in an intact state. Sacrificing your own well-being
is not a virtue, because you cannot then properly carry out your
obligations. This is why AA places sobriety first, even before family responsibilities, because if one does not have sobriety, one cannot do anything for the family.

"The show must go on" is also a value statement, subordinat-
ing everything else in the world to "the show," whatever that may
be, and it is a dangerous value statement. A student attending a
university in a small town went berserk, was "streaking" in the
nude, and had damaged several cars. I received a call from the local
chief of police saying that this young man was in jail, but that he
was obviously mentally ill and needed to be in a psychiatric facility. It would be necessary for his father to come and get him out of
jail and take him to Pittsburgh. The father, who was chairman of
the board of a large corporation, was in New York at a stockhold-
ers' meeting, and was unable to come for two days, resulting in the
young man spending two days in jail. The father's decision that
his show must go on at the expense of his son being in jail rather
than receiving treatment had a crushing impact on the young man.

The proper response to "the show must go on" is simply, "Why?"
To most people this question never occurs, for it is simply assumed
to be true. Challenging this principle may lead the individual to
reflect on its validity. In regard to treatment of alcoholism or drug
addiction, the assertion should be refuted. Insisting that treatment
must be promptly initiated says to the person, "You are more important than the show, yet you are not indispensable." This may
be the beginning of developing a healthier perspective on life.

10

Birds of a Feather

Many people do not have an identity other than that of their occupation. When asked to tell who he is, a person is more likely to say "I am a doctor" or "I am a lawyer" than "I am a loving, caring person." Thinking of oneself only by what one *does* rather than what one *is* can result in behavioral problems.

Case 12: Are We Only What We Do?

Arthur was a brilliant executive who had been hired away from his position as CEO to try to save a failing company. He indeed performed the economic miracle, bringing the company from the red to the black in three years. He spent endless hours at the office, and when not at the office played golf with other industrialists. He sat on several foundations and served as consultant to a number of firms. Arthur had time for everything, except to be home.

He did not drink, but was a compulsive eater, carrying more than 100 excessive pounds. His doctor had warned him that he was inviting a heart attack and suggested that he consult a psychiatrist, which he was reluctant to do.

Arthur's wife consulted me, concerned that he was eating himself to death. She described him as a wonderful, caring person, but one who seemed to care more for others than for his own family. "He's never at home. I can't ask him for advice on anything, but he'll always respond to a request for advice from some businessman. I guess when you're kind to the whole world, you're cruel to your own."

I eventually did get to see Arthur, and he was not a cruel person. Rather, he was an example of what I describe in my book *Life's Too Short* (1995) as "compartmentalization." Earlier I noted that many people who have attained positions of prominence are overachievers who exerted themselves to reach their positions in order to compensate for their fancied inadequacies. Some people have global feelings of inferiority and consider themselves unworthy or inadequate across the board. Others feel very adequate in one area but inadequate in everything else. Arthur was a person who was well aware of his excellence as a corporate executive. However, as a *person* he felt he was a loser, and did not see any redeeming features in his personality except for his profession. Hence, when he was at the office he was comfortable, but at home, where there were no meetings to conduct or business to operate, he felt he had nothing to offer. His wife may have indeed needed a shoulder, but he felt he did not have one for her to lean on. His children needed guidance, but he did not feel that he had anything to offer them in this regard.

There is a human "law of gravity" which is as immutable as the physical law of gravity. It states that a human being will gravitate to a position of maximum comfort or least discomfort. For example, if on a hot, muggy day, one had the choice of a cool, air-conditioned room or a room where the heat was suffocating, one would naturally choose the more comfortable room. This is precisely what Arthur did. The office was comfortable, because there he felt competent. Home was uncomfortable, not because his wife and children were too demanding, but because he felt he had nothing to offer them as a husband or father.

Many people spend long hours at the office. Occasionally this is justified, but quite often the extended presence at the office is because it is a more comfortable place to be.

Much unnecessary suffering results from compartmentalization. Arthur was a beautiful person as well as an excellent businessman, but he did not know it. His family was deprived of a loving husband and father. He had much to offer them but was unaware of it.

Arthur's obesity was ultimately lethal, resulting in a fatal heart attack at age 58. In her book *Fat is a Family Affair* Dr. Judy Hollis states that for the compulsive eater, food is a substitute for relationships. People who think poorly of themselves generally shun relationships because they anticipate being rejected. As with the family, so with friends, Arthur felt he had nothing to offer.

Compartmentalists tend to relate to one another: educators to educators, lawyers to lawyers, doctors to doctors, business people to business people. With their own kind they can talk shop, whereas with others, dead silence may occur after the topics of weather, sports, and politics have been exhausted. Heaven forbid that you'd find yourself in a position where you would have to talk about your feelings. Overachievers tend to avoid feelings like the plague, because most of their feelings are painful ones. So lawyers ski with lawyers, business people play golf with business people, and doctors socialize with doctors.

Overeaters are *doers*. They might be more appropriately referred to as human *doings* rather than human *beings*. To *be* is most uncomfortable, and frequently the discomfort of *being* results in recourse to a chemical to anesthetize oneself.

Overachievers are often lonely people. They socialize, but even if they are not alone they still tend to be lonely.

There is a difference between *aloneness* and *loneliness*. Aloneness is a physical state, where one is by oneself. Aloneness need not be uncomfortable, and indeed, people may desire periods of solitude for study, reflection, or simply relaxation. Loneliness, on the other hand, is an uncomfortable emotional state. A person can be in solitude and not be lonely, but can be in a crowded stadium with thousands of people, yet be very lonely. *Aloneness is where one does not have others, whereas loneliness is where one does not have oneself.* The alienation from self is a painful state.

Analysis of overachievers often reveals that in their childhood and formative years, they felt different from others, that everyone else was better than they. By achieving positions of authority or prominence, they were able to overcome these feelings of inferiority and feel superior to others. What is characteristic of overachievers is that they either felt less than or more than, but never equal to. Overachievers thus continue to feel that they don't belong, and the reason for the social inbreeding is that although they may not feel they belong with other human *beings*, they feel less uncomfortable with human *doings*. It is as though they belong to the doctors' club, the lawyers' club, the businessmen's club, but not to the human race.

Many alcoholics state that what they found desirable in alcohol was that it took away the feelings of alienation and made them feel that they belonged. Alcohol overcame the distressful feelings of loneliness. "I always felt better than or less than, but with alcohol I felt I belonged." Alcohol and drugs are thus great equalizers. One of the reasons for the effectiveness of the Twelve Step programs may be that they do not acknowledge social or professional status. Once a person enters an AA or NA room, it makes no difference whether he or she is rich or poor, highly educated or illiterate. Neither money nor degree can get anyone any special privileges in AA or NA, and the program thus replaces chemicals as a powerful equalizer.

Dr. R., a radiologist, states that his moment of truth occurred in a prison cell. He'd been arrested in a small town for drunk driving and had spent the night in jail. The jailor approached him, saying, "We got a call from your father. He says you're a doctor."

Dr. R. proudly rose to his full five-feet seven-inches and said, "Yes, I am a physician." The jailor sneered. "Well, you don't look like a doctor. To me you look like a drunk." Dr. R. revealed, "At that moment the artificial aura of being a doctor melted away. I was just a drunk, a broken-down human being. All previous efforts at getting me to accept my alcoholism had failed. That jailor cut through the façade and reached to the very core, where I lived. I was a human being after all."

There are some Twelve Step groups that are "specialty groups," consisting wholly of doctors, lawyers, or nurses. It is the consensus that these groups are useful for occasional attendance only, so that problems encountered during recovery that may relate to a specific situation may be discussed with others who have similar problems. However, exclusive attendance at specialty groups is discouraged since this exclusivity feeds the pathologic feelings of uniqueness.

The criticism may be raised that participation in AA/NA does not eliminate the feelings of exclusivity, but merely adds another set of feathers whereby people can flock together. Whereas previously a person was a lawyer who related only to lawyers, he is now an alcoholic who relates only to alcoholics.

Even if this were valid, there is still much to be said for involvement in the new peer group. As noted, social inbreeding allows people to interact according to what they do, and the communication consists largely of shop talk. In the Twelve Step program, the whole realm of feelings is opened up, and people relate according to what they *feel*. One can sit in on a "step meeting" where one of the Twelve Steps is discussed and not hear the words "alcohol" or "drugs" mentioned at all. The discussion has shifted to feelings, to behavior, and to character traits, issues equally applicable to non-chemically dependent people.

But it isn't necessary that recovering people socialize exclusively with other recovering people. The enhanced feeling of self that one attains in recovery eliminates the anticipation and fear of rejection, and enables a person to relate more comfortably to all people, even those with whom one has little in common. The only common ground that should be necessary for one to relate to another is that both are humans, and this is one of the rewards of recovery.

11

The Conspiracy of Silence

Denial is a major obstacle to the treatment of the alcoholic, especially the alcoholic physician. In my mind there are three kinds of denial that allowed me to prolong my excessive drinking and get into trouble with it: colleague denial, society's denial, and self denial.

I can best explain colleague denial by sharing with you five alcoholic case histories. These histories show that physicians do not like to, know how to, or want to make a diagnosis of alcoholism in a colleague. In all these examples, a physician-patient was admitted to a hospital with problems that were a direct result of alcoholism, but alcoholism was never mentioned. This was due, in part, to a lack of knowledge, to a well-intentioned desire to cover-up, and to the fear of legal embarrassment and/or confrontation. It could be said that these attending physicians were unknowing, unwitting, and unwilling.

Example 1 is that of a 27-year-old physician who was admitted to the hospital with a diagnosis of therapeutic misadventure due to rabies vaccine, manifested by arthritis, fever, and erythematous induration at injection sites. He had, indeed, been receiving rabies injections while taking care of a patient who had succumbed to rabies.

He was admitted to the hospital with a mild flare-up at the injection sites after a weekend of heavy drinking. The flare-up disappeared in twenty-four hours, but he maintained his hospitalization an extra four days by rubbing his thermometer on the pillowcase when the nurse wasn't looking and by holding his breath prior to her taking his pulse.

Example 2 describes a 31-year-old physician admitted to a hospital following an auto accident that occurred four miles from where he remembered getting into his car. The diagnosis:

- Concussion, brain
- Contusion, multiple, face and right knee
- Wound, lacerated, multiple, face and right knee, without artery or nerve involvement
- Strain, acute, cervical spine

Surgical procedures were performed on this physician. One of his colleagues removed a blood alcohol memo from his chart. The judge reduced the charge to careless driving.

Example 3 tells of a 34-year-old physician who was admitted to his own hospital for five days after a weekend of heavy drinking. The diagnosis: synovitis, right hip, etiology undetermined, improved during hospitalization. At the time his doctors found a uric acid of 15 mg.% and hypertension. They felt this young man might have a rare syndrome of hyperuricemia-hypertension and obtained a sample of his father's blood, as this was apparently a syndrome that ran in families. The final diagnosis was changed to: hyperuricemia, etiology undetermined, probable gout, treated, improved.

He was treated with bed rest: the best thing in the world for a hangover. Bed rest, pretty nurses running around, three meals a day, tranquilizers, and sleeping pills . . . excellent, inadvertent detox for an alcoholic who's feeling miserable.

Example 4 concerns a 38-year-old physician who passed out at a party on December 24, received CPR from a nurse at the party, and was rushed by ambulance to the hospital. The attending physician knew that his doctor-patient-friend was simply drunk on Christmas Eve. He sent him home the next morning with the following diagnosis (an attempt to help his colleague):

- Vaso-vagal syncope
- Myositis, left chest
- Flu syndrome

Example 5 describes a 40-year-old physician who was admitted to his own hospital as an emergency. Alcohol was obviously involved by sight and smell. He had attempted suicide by inserting a steak knife into his chest in the area of his heart. He required exploratory surgery, undergoing a laparotomy where the knife track was thought to have gone. It had not, so the doctors had to open his chest and found the knife track into, but not through, the myocardium. Some hemopericardium was present, however. This physician was signed out without any staff attempts at discussion or intervention. The final diagnosis stated factually:

- Diagnosis: Knife wound, left chest
- Operations: Exploratory laparotomy
                   Exploratory thoracotomy

In case you're wondering if I was the patient in any of these examples, I must tell you that all five examples are mine. Five hospitalizations in thirteen years. No intervention. Just good intentions.

I've spoken with my colleagues in recent years and none of them suspected that I was actually an alcoholic. I think they probably felt, "There but for the grace of God go I." No one put these cases together, including me. No one realized the seriousness of my situation because, as I said, my colleagues were unknowing, unwitting, and unwilling.

12

One Doctor's Story

Much of the theory discussed in earlier chapters is vividly illustrated in the moving autobiographical account that follows. This is a "lead" given by a prominent physician at a convention of International Doctors in Alcoholics Anonymous. Except for minor editing and elimination of identifying features, the address is essentially verbatim with all its incomparable beauty, sincerity, and gentle force.

Case 13: A Daddy That They're Proud Of

"Hi, everybody. My name is Malcolm, and I am an alcoholic. I am also a physician, and I am licensed to practice medicine and surgery. I am married, and I have a family.

Now you'll notice I say that I am an alcoholic first. This is the way I live, and this is the way I conduct all of my affairs, because I know that if at anytime I should forget I'm an alcoholic, then I go back to what I was. I was the most lonely, miserable, lost, sick, sorry, suffering human being that you could imagine. But I don't have to be that way anymore. I don't have to be that way today. Of course, I am sorry for some of the things that happened, especially the people that I hurt; but I don't have to be ashamed of me today. I don't have to be ashamed of me and my actions and my deeds. I've come to realize that wherever I am, wherever I might be, if I am with you people, then this is where I belong—because you are my people, the people that took me in when I had nothing and had lost everything—you were the people that loved me back to health and to sanity. Yes, you restored my soul, and you gave me everything that I have today. Before I go any further, I'd just like to take this opportunity to thank you for the privilege of being here.

I went to my first IDAA meeting in 1968. I didn't go back until the meeting in 1974 at the Breakers, and I am awfully sorry about all of those I missed in between. But at this particular point in time, there is absolutely no question in my mind that I am exactly where I am supposed to be and I am doing exactly what I am supposed to be doing, and this is a wonderful way to live my life. At one time I was so well known as the drunk Dr. ————— that I got fired from the practice of medicine. I will never forget the anguish that I went through trying to get up enough courage when I was finally asked to come back to that hospital after I had come into the program of AA. I remember driving down there, and I had to drive around the block two or three times until I finally got up enough courage to go in. As I walked across that lot, I looked up at those buildings, and I knew that all of those people were looking down at me. I wanted to run and I wanted to hide, and I never have wanted to just completely get away from anything as much in my life.

Now I go back in that hospital every day and several other hospitals too, and I am anxious to meet the people and talk to them, and I am anxious to tell them how I got the way I am today. They knew me as I once was, and I am certainly not ashamed of the way I am today. If they do ask me I'll tell them. I'll tell them about you people, I'll tell them about this program, I'll tell them about the fellowship of Alcoholics Anonymous and the one thing I think we have that far surpasses anything I have ever found in any organization in this life, and that is best expressed by the simple four letter word, LOVE. The love one alcoholic shares with another alcoholic. I am so grateful to you, but if we were to talk about gratitude today, I am afraid we'd be here most of the day, and I do want to get on with the story. I do believe in telling what it used to be like, what happened, and the way it is today.

My father was a doctor, and my mother was a teacher and a Sunday school instructor. Being a teacher, she realized that I wasn't the smartest thing that had ever come this way, so she spent a lot of extra time with me. She taught me how to study, how to concentrate, and this enabled me to go a long way. She also instilled in me a very deep and a very strong spiritual foundation from which I was later to turn away—to turn away from the God of my childhood.

I went to school and we had a happy home. We had a very close and very warm family. I took my first drink when I was about 5 years old. Now I had the whooping cough, when as most of you know it was a real serious condition and a lot of people died of it. One night I ran down the hall, and I grabbed my daddy around his legs, and I stood there just racking in this spasm of coughing. He took me in the bathroom and stood me up on the sink and poured down about that much whiskey in me. Immediately the coughing stopped. So you see my very first experience with alcohol had filled a need. It gave me relief, and it released my pain— I could sleep, and probably the rest of the family could sleep too.

Now I don't think that's got a thing in the world to do with me being an alcoholic, but I think it's interesting. What is important is the fact that I remember it so well. You see this is something that happened about forty-four years ago, and I remember it just like it was yesterday—daddy took me in, stood me up on the sink, and poured out that much alcohol, and I drank it right down. I do believe that something happens when this catalyst is added to our personalities or to our chemistries. Just think of how many times you hear drunkalogs being related, and people go into minute details describing their very first drink!

Anyhow, I went to school and was able to do real well. I made good grades, and I was usually at the top of my class, not because I was so smart, but because my mother had taught me how to study. I was to lose her in my teens. She had a form of paralysis, and this was a tremendous loss to me. I became very much alone. Now, somewhere along the age of twelve, I remember my first experience of feeling different from other people just knowing that I was different. I was different from you; I was different from normal folks. Oh, I could wear the same clothes or have the same kind of toys, baseball glove, or a bicycle, but yet I and my things were different from other people, and I was alone. With my father being a doctor and gone from home most of the time, my sister considerably older, and my mother being very ill, I was alone, alone and different from other people.

At this point in my life, I started to search to find the place where I'd be accepted, a place where I'd belong, a place to be needed. Oh, I know my folks loved me, they loved me as much, I guess, as anybody could; but this wasn't enough, and I certainly never did feel needed. I finished high school—there was some drinking in high school but no problem drinking. I went to college, and there were no problems there, either.

Finally, I was accepted to medical school. Now, this was a goal and I had achieved it. Ever since my earliest recollection, I knew exactly what I wanted to do; I wanted to grow up and be a doctor like my father, and I wanted to work with my father, and I had set my sights on this goal. By being accepted into medical school, perhaps I had achieved this and so I began to relax. I began to drink more and more and more. As a result, my grades deteriorated, and I fell from the upper top of the class to the lower third, I don't know how low. They were kind and they didn't tell you about that, but I finally graduated in the lower third of the class.

I was accepted as an intern at a large city hospital, and since those were the early war years, there was a tremendous shortage—a manpower shortage and also a doctor shortage. We had only four surgery interns for that whole hospital. Now this is important, because when we worked, we worked thirty-six hours on and twelve hours off. You know the things that you remember, going from operating room to operating room and staying in the suture line for twenty-four hours. When the twelve hours off came, I was so exhausted that I would go home, eat, and then go to bed, so I didn't drink. Also, by working with these people, the indigent people there, I wasn't much, but I was all they had, and they appreciated it. Maybe this was satisfying some sort of need in me that up until then I hadn't felt. I don't know why, but I stopped drinking during this period. I think this was purely a stopgap in the progression of my disease of active alcoholism.

I finished my internship in general surgery, and then I went into my specialty. I am a specialist in obstetrics and gynecology and a Fellow in the American College of Obstetricians and Gynecologists. I am very proud of this, and I am very proud of the training that I received.

We know that God didn't mean for man to live alone, and after I was in training and in my specialty, He brought me a beautiful blue-eyed, brown-haired girl, and I wasn't alone anymore. You see, I had somebody to love me; I had somebody to care for me; I had somebody to laugh with, somebody to cry with, somebody to share with, somebody who belonged to me and somebody who I belonged to. I hadn't remembered a relationship like this since my earliest childhood, so my whole world turned around. I finished my training. We got married and then I was drafted. We drove out to Fort Sam Houston, Texas. As most of you know, that's where they send doctors to make soldiers out of them, but they didn't have any intention of making me a soldier, anyhow. This was nothing but a six-week vacation with pay. The pay thing was important, too, because those five years I was in residency, all we got was $10 a month and all the milk we could drink. That was it. But now in the army, you see, I'm an officer and a gentleman. I'm entitled to a salary, I have somebody who loves me, I have a companion, and I don't feel different, I'm certainly not alone, and this is one of the happiest times of my life. I'll always remember it that way. Oh, there was some drinking, but out there, there was drinking around the clock. There were parties everywhere—you never had to look for one, you were usually right in the middle of one. But this was no problem, and we had a lot of fun. I enjoyed army life very much.

The six weeks ended though, and I received orders to go to France. Now the honeymoon was over. Everything was still secure, the shooting war had just ended, but it was still secure and my wife couldn't go, so the honeymoon was over and I was alone again. I never did get to France; all my bags and baggage did, but I didn't. I got to Fort Dix, was rerouted, and called down to the Pentagon. There I received new orders—a coincidence.

It seems the commanding general of a large army post in Virginia had a wife who was expecting a baby, and I was the only one available to handle this military emergency, so when I got to the Pentagon I was reassigned to an army post in Virginia. My wife and I drove down to the beautiful Shenandoah Valley. My whole world turned around again. The birds were singing, the grass was green, the sky was blue, and my life had just lit up. We pulled into the post and as the MPs snapped to attention, I said, "Boy, this is a Class A outfit here." Well, from the moment I drove through those gates, I was the commanding general's wife's doctor. Wherever the commanding general went, the commanding general's wife went, and the so did her doctor. We took the helicopter to New York for the weekend, commanding general, commanding general's wife, commanding general's wife's doctor. Wherever the commanding general and his lady went, the little doctor went too. This is a really wonderful, swinging way to spend time in the army.

I have to say, though, that she had a nice baby boy, who I am sure will be a commanding general someday as were his father and grandfather, and this will have to be my contribution to the defense of the United States. I really did enjoy army life, and these were very nice folks. I probably would have stayed in the army, except for this desire, this feeling of duty, ambition, or calling, whatever you want, to work with my father. I left the army to work with my dad. Now here is the picture: I'm a native son, born and raised. My father had a large practice, an excellent reputation; I've been to school, medical school, graduate school; they just rolled out the carpet there when I returned, and they gave me jobs and positions and committees. People were doing all these things just as I thought they should (since by now my ego was out of sight), all except for my father. As far as he was concerned, I was just like anybody else, and he wasn't about to turn over the care and treatment of his patients, these people that he loved so much, to me until he found out where I was. He never left me alone; he stayed right with me, and I resented this. I resented it very much. It took me many years to realize that he wasn't constantly supervising me. He simply wanted to be with me, but I resented it; I resented having him looking over my shoulder. Here I was a young hero who had received the finest training returning from the war. I was ready to come in, take over, and put the old man out to pasture, but he wouldn't do that.

Now my wife was starting to have babies and I resented it— I resented those babies coming along and interfering with this romance, this love affair that I had. I resented those children. I resented the intrusion into my life. I resented her for having them (I guess I thought she did it all by herself). But now I turned away, completely away from the only two people in this world who really loved me or who really cared for me. As a result of that, I began to build up my wall—a wall of dishonesty, lying, cheating, hiding, and resenting—all of the things that make it up. I began to drink and continued to drink more and more and more. I had drunk a lot in the Army, but that was not problem drinking, that was fun drinking most of the time. It was at this point I entered into the serious drinking of alcoholism.

There is absolutely no question in my mind that at this particular time I crossed over that invisible, but completely irreversible, line into the disease of active alcoholism. And this is a line that, once you cross it, you don't ever go back. Early on in the game, I heard my friend Billy say, "Once a cucumber becomes a pickle, it doesn't ever go back to being a cucumber again." By now I was well pickled, and this is when I entered into my alcoholic career. I was doing a lot of things I shouldn't have been doing; I was working, staying away from home, and doing all the things that alcoholics do. Living this kind of life, something had to happen—and it did. On Monday morning, October 1, 1962, I had a massive heart attack.

I was taken to the hospital, and for a while they didn't know if I would live. Then I didn't know if I would ever be able to work again. I became very depressed and very bitter, and this is when I also turned against my God—the God of my childhood. "Why did You do this thing to me, to cast me down helpless, lying here on the bed when I had just gotten to the point of being of service to myself and to mankind? Lying helpless here, not being able to bathe myself, the height of indignity. Why did You do this thing to me?" I wouldn't even let them open the blinds in the room; it might let the sunlight in. Leave me alone in my grief. Can't you see how I suffer? Leave me alone, leave me alone!

Looking back on it now, this was nothing other than the good Lord reaching down, grabbing me up, giving me a good shake, sitting me back down and saying, "Now look, who are you, where did you come from and where are you going?" A wonderful chance to get out of the rat race, to regroup, all expenses paid, and all excuses made. Examine your life! I got absolutely no benefit out of this opportunity, only bitterness.

I finally left the hospital and went down to live with my sister on a small island off the coast of Georgia. Now I want to take a minute to tell you all about that, and if you ever get a chance, I want you to go there—it plays a tremendous part in my recovery. It's a beautiful little island off the coast; it's very green and very pretty, and as you drive across the last bridge, one of the first things you're impressed with are the massive trees—the tall and stately pines, the huge live oaks that are so many feet around in circumference. The boughs are as big as trees themselves, and the limbs go down almost to the ground, and then they lift up their branches in supplication to the heavens. There's Spanish moss in the tops of these trees and as the wind blows the moss dances, and you can hear the music. There's a tremendous sensation of peace in this whole area. I'm not the only one that feels this way; I want you to go there. Nothing to me personifies strength any more than those great giant oak trees. When you see it, you'll understand.

While there I regained my health. I came back and I went back to work and quickly fell into the same habits as before. You see, nothing had changed and nothing had altered in my life. You know, anybody who has any trouble with his heart is not supposed to get nervous. You are supposed to sleep eight to twelve hours every night, so I had tranquilizers to keep me calm, and sleeping pills to make sure that I slept, and alcohol to dilate my coronary blood vessels. I don't think they meant for me to take them all at the same time, but I did!

This is why I feel qualified to speak on just about any form of addiction you want to talk about, because I took everything there was at that time. I took everything except Miles Nervene and Lydia Pinkham and I would have taken them too if they had come in free samples. All I had to do was just open the desk drawer and there it was. I do want to say a word or two, though, about these drugs because I think it's the greatest thing that faces many of us. I am a total addict. I could get addicted to anything, I think, but all of us have a drug of choice. I don't care what you call these things, sedatives, mood elevators, antidepressants, tranquilizers, uppers, downers, and even tricyclics that make you go all three ways. These have proved addicting to me, an alcoholic, and I feel very strongly that they are addicting to all other alcoholics. If at any time that I choose to start taking any of these, I'm not going to fool around for long with Elavil, Dexamyl, Dalmane, Ativan, Tranxene, Serax, Valium, Librium or any of these. I'm going to go to the one that I want the most, the one that I'm going to end up with anyhow, and that's going to be Scotch whiskey. But it's going to be a swimming pool-full, because that's what it will take. I know I can get drunk again, but I don't think I have another getting sober. I think this is the last time around for me, and I respect that very much.

I got back into my work and one night they called me to come down to the hospital because they had a real bad emergency down there. I got dressed, got in my car, and raced down the expressway with my ego running wild, sort of hoping a policeman might stop me. "I'm a doctor on emergency, you know." So I pull into the emergency room, and I leave the motor running and the lights on, and I open the car door and I go through those emergency room doors, a sort of combination Superman and Walter Mitty. Have no fear, if I am here! Well, actually the case went well, and everything would have been fine if I had kept my mouth shut, but I had to tell them how lucky they were to have me down there, and I did that at some length.

The next morning when I came to work, there were people around in little groups whispering to each other and looking at me. Now, whenever they're doing that, they're talking about you, and you know they're talking about you because you can feel it right here. It didn't take long to find out why they were talking about me. I was called to the administrator's office and told never to return to that hospital again under the influence of alcohol. Well, I had sobered up enough to keep my mouth shut, so I went out, got in my car, and drove over to my office filled with righteous indignation. Why, these were the most narrow-minded, unappreciative people you'd ever seen. Here I had gotten up in the middle of the night to save that woman's life, and they're talking about those two or three little drinks I had and maybe a sleeping pill or two. I reached under the seat and got a hot vodka bottle. My friends, there is nothing quite like hot vodka. It sends chills up my spine right now, but it does have authority. I took a couple of drinks out of the vodka bottle and drove over to my office.

By now, my father had heard about this. My father was probably one of the kindest men that ever walked the face of this earth. He was about my height with white hair and beautiful blue-gray eyes. He came in the back door, walked up to me, and looked at me. I saw those eyes just mist over; I saw him look at me, and I saw the pain. I knew what he wanted to say. He wanted to say, "Go home son, go home," but he didn't. He came over, put his arm around me, and stayed with me. He always stayed with me.

Anyhow, I went on working, and as it often happens to us alcoholics, I kept falling up the stairs. I kept getting promotions, and getting put on committees, and my father was giving me more responsibilities. He knew something was going on, but he didn't know what it was, and our communications weren't good at all. Certainly, they weren't any good at home, but I kept getting promoted. Finally, I got on the executive committee of the whole hospital. They called me to come down to the executive committee meeting, and it was to be my first one. They never called anybody else to make sure that they were coming, and I don't know why they chose to call me (and if any of you know, I don't think I want you to tell me). Usually, they just sent a notice—but anyhow, they called me. I got up that morning to go to the meeting, and it was very cold. It was in December right before Christmas, and I got fully dressed, suit, overcoat, muffler, hat, gloves, and dark glasses. This was before daylight! I got there a little late—they were all sitting around talking and all of a sudden everything stopped. I walked across the room and sat down, and once again, they all started looking at me. I knew they were looking at me, and I didn't know what to do. There really wasn't anything to do, so I passed out!

This really shook them up. They knew I had trouble with my heart, and they said, "Oh my Lord, he's dead!" One great big fellow reached down and picked me up and had me up in his arms while they were pulling my collar out. They were knocking over chairs and bells were ringing and sirens were going and I was coming in and out of consciousness and saying, "Please let this be a dream, please let this be a dream." It wasn't a dream. Finally, I woke up, and they had me in an oxygen tent. They had something hooked up to everything you could hook up something to. I mean everything! There I was and they were coming in, so kind, so solicitous. Then the specialists started arriving—the learned men of medicine, friends of mine, friends of my father's. They listened to my heart and they looked at the heart tracings, and they frowned. There wasn't anything wrong with the heart—I was a medical mystery!

I solved the mystery for them. I went into the DTs. I heard things and I saw things and I hired people and I fired people. This was a Catholic hospital; it was almost Christmas, and they had Christmas carols and trees, and nuns, and angels—some of it was real and some of it wasn't! But it was all real to me, and I tried running up and down the halls in that little outfit they give you that doesn't quite cover everything, and I had nuns and nurses and orderlies and doctors after me. We'd go down this hall, and we'd come back up that hall. It was a real experience. I woke up one morning, though, and got my things together. They said, "What are you doing?" and I said, "I'm going home." They said, "You can't do that, you've been too sick. You've had this trouble with your heart." I said, "Look, I know my rights. This is a hospital, not a jail, and I'm going home to be with my children for Christmas."

They said, "All right, but will you talk to your doctors?" and I said, "Yes, just get them down here."

They called for these men, these wonderful men, my friends, and tried to reason with me, but there was no reasoning with me. They called my father and said, "You've got to come and get him, you've got to do something with him." My father called my wife and they came to get me and took me to the local drunk hospital. They drove me over there and I was admitted. This father of mine, this man who had taught me more about medicine than was ever written in any medical textbook; this man who taught me to put the heart in the art of medicine; who taught me love and compassion, and always to maintain the dignity of every human being; this man who loved me more than any father ever loved a son, had to see me admitted. I was truly the apple of his eye. When I think of the pain, the suffering, and the embarrassment that I caused him, it's more than I can bear. But bear it I must and share it I will, along with the experiences that I had there.

I don't remember much about it. I remember entering the hospital, but they gave me more and more drugs and more and more medication, until I completely lost my mind. They did all the wrong things that you could possibly do for an alcoholic, I think. Of the things I do remember, none are pleasant. I remember being strapped down to a table all night long. I remember the pain in my back after convulsions. I remember being held; I remember being placed in a straight jacket; I remember looking down at my fingers and seeing the blood encrusted around my nails from trying to claw my way out of the closet where I was hiding from whatever it was that was after me. I remember the screams, I remember the fears—and may I never forget it, may I never forget it. This is why I say with all sincerity that I promise everyone that I will do everything in this world I can to keep you from going through what I went through.

I finally did leave that hospital and once again went down to the island to visit my sister, to live and to recover. I would go out on the beach and I would walk. Some wonderful things happened. I didn't drink and I didn't take any drugs; I was numb from all the chemicals, but now something began to happen inside of me. I would sit under the great oak tree and realize the strength that was there, and oh, how I wished to embrace this tree and say, "Give me some of your strength." I experienced a feeling of peace that I had never known before—unless perhaps when my mother held me in her arms. I was safe. As best as I can describe, it was the absence of fear. Fear is the emotion common to every alcoholic. I've never seen an alcoholic who wasn't scared to death.

I would walk along the beach, I would listen to the birds and the ocean. Next time you're at the ocean, think about it. Listen to the mighty ocean roar; it is a controlled force, a divine source of power. There is no question in your mind as you see the waves go out that another wave will come back in, and as you sit on the bridges and watch the whitecaps and the birds in flight and the little fiddler crabs and the fish in the sea, something happens. Something began to happen inside of me. I knew that as long as I stayed there I would be safe, but of course, I had to go back to work.

I didn't even know if I would have a job or not. You know, when you go into the DTs there isn't much of a secret about what's wrong with you. My friends in the medical profession almost killed me. They said, "We want you to come back and we want you to go back to work, but keep it under control." Keep it under control? There wasn't any control! I couldn't go two hours without having a drink and knowing what was going to happen—this is the horror of alcoholism: the running, the hiding, the lying, the cheating, the living in fear, the feeling of doom and impending disaster. The next step you take, you're going to fall off a cliff. The telephone rings. Who is it? What do they want? They've come to get you! Keep it under control? There wasn't any control! I went back to my hospital but they sent me back home. I received a letter the next morning saying, "Don't ever come back to this hospital. You're fired." I was humiliated and disgraced.

Once again I went back to my island and I was introduced to a program called Alcoholics Anonymous. I wasn't ready for it at that time, but I did go to a meeting. I went to a meeting for all the wrong reasons, purely and simply to get people off my back. I remember they gave out these little poker chips. I picked up one that had the initials AA on it. I went home, woke up my sister, gave it to her and said, "Look here, I joined AA." I hadn't joined AA. I used AA for all the wrong reasons. I did go back to work, and several people tried to work with me but I wouldn't let them. I couldn't let them know me, I couldn't let them know how miserable and rotten a person I was inside. "No—I don't need you, leave me alone."

Finally, one night when things were pretty bad, my wife called this AA fellow to come to the house and talk to me—he's now my sponsor. He's a really big guy, six-and-a-half-feet tall and weighs about 250 pounds. He's also a finger pointer. He came in and started talking to me. "We know what you're doing. This is a program of honesty. You're taking these drugs and you're going to the meetings, and you're not fooling anyone." I wasn't ready for all that, and I rose up to all five feet and said, "Now listen. What gives you the right to come in here, in my home and talk to me like this? Here I am, a man with two college degrees, two cars in the carport, and bank accounts in two different banks. I'm an upstanding member of the community and I go to church every Sunday morning." He said, "You remember that when the sheriff comes out here to get you."

Once again, a little knowledge is a dangerous thing, so I said, "By the way, I didn't call you to come out here and help me. You have no right to do this." But notice I didn't say "don't try." He hung his head and walked to the door. Immediately I realized I had the advantage. I was just like a little feisty dog; I'd get him every time he slowed down. I'd nip him and finally back him into a corner. It was sort of like David and Goliath, and I went through all of this again and I said, "Why do you do this? Do you do this because you hate me?" This is where this man brought me the eleventh commandment—I refer to John 13: 34 where it is written, "A new commandment I give unto you, love thy brother." He said, "No, it's not because I hate you, it's because I love you." Here was this six-and-a-half-foot giant, standing there in my kitchen telling me that he loves me after he'd said all of those other things about me! I couldn't comprehend this.

I wish that I could say I stopped drinking right then, but I didn't. It was two days later. Two days later I went into the living room, a room we seldom use, and there was something inside of me, perhaps my last grasp of sanity. I was able to go through a complete destruction and dissolution of ego. I became entirely willing and ready to turn my will and my life over to the care of God as best as I could at that time. I fell on my knees and I said, "God help me. God help me now." I had prayed many times before, "God, get me out of this, God, do that for me one more time, God, please get me through this." Bargains, pleadings, promises, but this time, "Show me the way, please show me the way."

Immediately I remembered a man I'd heard of before, a doctor who'd had a problem similar to mine. I called him and within two hours I walked into his house and into his home. I am speaking about Dr. John. Dr. John and his wife opened their home to me and took me in. In addition to these people, whom I love so very much, were people just like you. You took me in, you put your arms around me, you loved me, you knew I was lonely and you knew I was afraid. You knew I was sick and you knew I was worried, and that I was bankrupt. You didn't ask me who I was or where I came from or what I had done. You said, "It's going to be all right, just walk with us." You took me into your homes and into your hearts, and you gave me everything that I have today.

Many things happened while I was down there, too many to go into. But finally, one morning I was standing there looking out of the French doors in the den—it was November and the warm sunlight was coming in, and I experienced a feeling of peace that completely passed through me from head to toe. And accompanying that peace and the sensation of warmth was the instant realization which I knew then and I know now, that at that moment I was within the presence of God, and as long as I remained so, it would not be necessary for me to take a drink or a pill again. I was free— I was free at last!

I left after a little while and came back home. I started going to meetings, I started getting active in my practice and I started treating alcoholics after my regular office hours. When I'm gone from home, I'm busy doing work and going to meetings. My whole life has turned around. My family is a happy family, my home is a happy home, and my father is once again enjoying my working with him.

Finally, one Sunday afternoon, I came home—I'm still gone from home much of the time, and my children were out in the yard playing catch, and they looked up and saw me. I had probably changed shirts or something and they said, "Hi Dad, where are you going?" I said, "I'm going to a meeting." I saw them look at each other, and then I saw them look go back around and I knew that they were thinking, "Come on out and play with us, Daddy; come on out and be with us for a while." They looked at each other, they looked at their mother, and then they looked back at me and said, "Have a good time, Daddy, I love you, Daddy, I'll see you in the morning, Daddy."

I got into my car and I drove for a little while, but I had to stop, because I realized what these children had told me. I hope you realize it now, too, because this is the message I want you to carry with you. These are the children who had been afraid. These are the children who used to hide from me. These are the children who used to cry all night, "What's wrong with Daddy? Where is Daddy? Why don't we have a daddy like other kids?" These are the children who were ashamed; these are the children I abused (thank God never physically). "Where is Daddy, what's wrong with Daddy now? Is Daddy back in the hospital?" These are the children who had to help their mother pick me up and put me in bed. "Why doesn't Daddy ever go to the little league games?" or "Mother, please don't let Daddy come," which is even worse. But now it was, "Have a good time, Daddy, I love you, Daddy, I'll see you in the morning, Daddy." Why? Because they have a daddy now. They've got a daddy they love and are proud of.

I never will forget one day looking out of the window and seeing my beautiful little girl walking up the hill from the school bus, her fist clenched, chin against her chest, tears coming down her cheeks, because on the school bus they had called her daddy a drunk. This is the same little girl who just drove us to the airport. She put her arms around my neck and said, "Make a good talk, Daddy and thank them, Daddy." She's a sophomore in college now.

"But for the Grace of God"—what does that mean to you? I'll tell you what it means to me. It is a gift from God that I did not deserve. Yes, my friends, I consider myself well-blessed and filled with God's grace. I want to thank You as my children do, and I want to thank You especially for the fact that my father lived long enough to see me regain my place in the medical profession, not only as a gynecologist but also in the field of alcoholism and addiction. (He never could say AA, though, he always said, "AAA.") This gives me the right and the privilege to say, "Thank God for these things," for the difference in me that led me to the disease of alcoholism and drug addiction, to the program of Alcoholics Anonymous and to you wonderful people. If it weren't for that I wouldn't be here today, and I wouldn't be what I am today. I am a grateful alcoholic. I feel very humble to be in your presence. I want to thank you all, and I want to thank Dr. John and his wife and my wife. Most of all, I want to say, "Thank You" to the God of my understanding. How great Thou art!

13

A Dentist's Story

Some people seem to be able to snatch failure right out from the jaws of success. With everything going for them, they manage to bungle things, and of course, nothing can do that as well as drinking or drugging. Fortunately, when the magic of recovery takes place, they can often reverse the course and even make up for lost time.

Case 14: Laughing Gas—No Laughing Matter

My name is Malcolm and I'm an alcoholic and poly-addicted. It is my belief that both the egg and the sperm that were united in my conception in February 1935, were under the influence of nicotine, caffeine, and alcohol. However, another significant historical event occurred on June 10, 1935 (during my gestation period), namely the founding of Alcoholics Anonymous. It resulted in the establishment of a program that provides a spiritual path to recovery from addictive diseases. This Twelve Step Program, in one form or another, has spread throughout most of the world.

My birth occurred on November 20, 1935 and it took me exactly fifty-one years to the day to acquire the spirituality of that path. Two of today's prominent authors, John Bradshaw and Dr. Wayne Dier, in their respective writings, suggest that we are spiritual beings on a human journey. I was apparently a human being on a spiritual journey. Through the concepts of dysfunctional family relationships and understandings of what it means to be a shame-based person, I perceive my life today and its purpose in a new and inspirational way. In Twelve Step programs, self-disclosure is telling others what happened to you and what it's like for you today.

Essentially, I grew up in an environment that enabled me to addictively use mood-altering substances and behaviors. I developed a projected false personality. I went crazy. I struggled with psychiatric help and found sobriety through Alcoholics Anonymous. Today I live with a heaven within.

Alcohol, nicotine, and caffeine consumption was a constant in my nuclear and extended family through my formative years. After all, it was the Second World War and anyone who wanted to be someone smoked, drank, and swore with panache. My brother, half-sister, and I assumed our respective roles—lost child, scapegoat, and mascot. My addictions to mood-altering substances and behaviors came early and fast—chocolate, colas, and movies by the age of 5, nicotine at age 6, caffeine and sexual climaxes by age 8, alcohol at age 9, and nitrous-oxide at age 28. Fortunately, I did not develop relationships with the uppers, downers, and all-arounders of the '60s, '70s, and '80s.

Briefly my life patterns emerged as follows: I became accomplished in lying, cheating, stealing, manipulating, and fighting by 7 years of age. Behavior patterns resulted in my failing first grade, seventh grade, and making the honor roll in ninth grade, and finally graduating 105th in a class of 125 in high school. I was always trying to pattern myself after whoever seemed to be most important at the time.

During my teen years, under heavy use of alcohol, I was burdened with the mental anguish of "what shall I become?"—a swashbuckling white-scarfed jet pilot or a professional man like my father, the dentist. My high school counselor suggested I try a labor trade. I struggled with college for three years while working part time, being in love, smoking, and binge drinking whenever needed as a coping mechanism. I avoided the draft by maintaining sufficient grades to preserve my deferment. My heroes while I was growing up were the men who fought in World War II. I always dreamed I would one day be a warrior.

Through the grace of God and periodic cheating on my part and a desire to be somebody, I matriculated into dental school and found my niche. I had also taken the entrance examination for the Naval Air Cadets and passed it without cheating. But I decided to set that career aside. Classmates I associated with in dental school were recent veterans of the Korean conflict, and the person I sat beside for four years had been a jet pilot. We all worked part time, studied, smoked, partied on 200 proof, stolen hospital alcohol, and were married and raising children. We became experts in cheating our way through dental school, both on our exams and our lives. With the help of alcohol and nicotine I graduated cum laude and eighth in the class of 1961.

I entered the U.S. Navy when martinis and manhattans were ten cents each during happy hour. I had developed the attitude that I deserved a party break as an officer and a gentleman after all my efforts. Three months before my scheduled release from active duty, I took a course and was introduced to nitrous-oxide analgesia. This precipitated a manic phase in my life that lasted until I was psychiatrically hospitalized for acting out the day before my release from active duty. Under the influence of a very excessive amount of alcohol, I had manipulated my way onto an aircraft carrier that was going out to sea, and then tried to persuade the pilots to take me for a ride in a jet plane while still in a very manic state. By completely disrobing in a public place to try to put on a pilot's uniform, I had apparently convinced the powers that be that I needed psychiatric hospitalization. (I was AWOL from my dental clinic.)

After my release from the navy and psychiatric counseling, which took nearly four months, I did not drink alcohol or smoke for over a year. I was establishing my private practice and never in my life had been so full of fears, insecurities, and doubts. During a hunting trip with my father and a friend with whom I had first started smoking as a child, I again used alcohol and nicotine. It felt as though my fears were gone and the old Malcolm was back. Throughout my professional career in the '60s, '70s, and early '80s, I tried to understand what was occurring in my life. Upon reflecting on my life, it seemed as though every seven years I would act out, get into trouble, or be out of touch with reality and have to consult with my psychiatrist. In 1970, under the excessive use of vodka and also in deep emotional pain and guilt feelings for my adulterous behavior, I realized what the combination of emotional and physical pain could do. I then had an emergency appendectomy and I could remember hoping as I was going under the anesthetic that I would not come out again. I came to believe that I had psychiatric problems and was a functional alcoholic.

In the fellowship of AA, people speak of spiritual experiences. I had one in 1971. During self-administration of nitrous-oxide to relax at the end of a very tough day, I was alone in my office and had set the flow meters on my nitrous machine rather high. I was in a rather dreamy state, as I recall, and then I felt immediate embarrassment when my father touched me on the shoulder and whispered in my ear to turn down the nitrous-oxide and flush myself with oxygen. As my head cleared and my senses returned, an overwhelming feeling came over me and a chill ran the length of my spine. This was the summer of 1971 and my father had died

in my arms in 1966. I never self-administered nitrous-oxide after
that.

During the middle '70s I had taken courses on nutrition and read
about how certain hospitals would use large doses of niacin to treat
chronic alcoholics. I began taking megadoses of niacin and other
vitamins to try and control my alcoholism and eliminate my occasional nicotine addiction. With the death of my mother in 1982,
my other personalities seemed to emerge more often. This was the
part of me that enjoyed being away from my family and professional life and doing some real drinking and smoking and male
bonding.

On one such occasion in a restaurant in Annapolis, while male
bonding and under the influence of many manhattans, I acted out
in rage, got into a street fight, and finally wound up in jail. The
fight was actually pleasurable and apparently released a lot of
stifled emotions. During the shameful aftermath of my actions,
my attorney suggested that I consult with an alcohol counselor
to determine if indeed I might be alcoholic and establish a line of
defense for the judge. I consulted with a patient in my practice
whom I'd known since grade school and who counseled alcoholics. At her suggestion, I was to attend a Caduceus meeting. I took
my last drink of alcohol and smoked my last cigarette at 5:30 pm
on Saturday, November 8, 1986 because I was to see my patient,
the counselor, on Monday, November 10 and I wanted to be sober
and try to prove to her that I really wasn't that much of an alcoholic. After my consultation, I continued not to drink or smoke as
I had on many occasions before. On November 20, 1986, my 51st
birthday, I attended my first Caduceus meeting with a colleague
in the profession and my wife of twenty-eight years. During that
meeting I heard other physicians and dentists reveal their psychiatric hospitalizations and struggles with alcohol and other drugs.
I heard my life being repeated by others. The person who removed
my appendix in 1970 was also there. When it came time for me to
speak, I said "My name is Malcolm, and I'm an alcoholic." What-

ever words followed, I do not recall because I could feel myself undergoing another spiritual change. It was the now familiar tingling sensation of the entire spinal column and a clearing feeling throughout my brain.

During my life I had developed the belief that I was alcoholic and had even disclosed that belief to numerous other people. But apparently my true self had never fully accepted that belief. My false self acted as the denial barrier. When I self-disclosed to a group of mostly strangers with the same disease, my Higher Power released my obsession and compulsion for mood-altering drugs, alcohol, and nicotine, and acceptance for me had finally become a reality. As it is written in the Big Book of Alcoholics Anonymous, I've been rocketed into the Fourth Dimension, and I found much of Heaven. My life over the past seven years, living one day at a time and enjoying one moment at a time, appears blissful. I continue to seek support through the Twelve Step programs and read, study, and memorize information about my disease. And now with complete reliance on a power greater than myself, I realize I don't have to cheat on exams or other challenges to obtain what I think I need. I am now more a human being rather than a human doing. I have come to believe that I am a spiritual being on a human journey rather than a human being on a spiritual journey.

Living in recovery has given me more rewards than I could possibly verbalize. Physically, I have far greater reserve energy than fifteen or twenty years ago. My vital signs are in an ideal range, and I am more aware of the subtle signs of health and well-being of my body. Of course the pain of hangovers is no more, or the arthritic-type joint pain that was apparent after the second or third day of heavy drinking. No more tachycardia echoing in my ears while waiting to fall asleep. My sleep is more restful and revitalizing. Through my dreams I hope to enhance my spiritual life. Emotionally, I am aware of an eternal sea of serenity that was never with me in my addictions. Intellectually, by continuing to educate myself about my disease, I am gaining an understanding of the concepts associated with the disease, such as the first, second, and third stages of recovery or original pain work and examining my own codependency, family of origin issues, and slowly discovering and nurturing my inner child. Because of my background I realize that too often I am probably in my head and need to focus more on my emotions. Professionally, I have attained a greater degree of satisfaction than I have known in many years. I believe my Higher Power has given me an awareness and a consciousness that is beneficial to colleagues who may be struggling with chemical dependency. Spiritually, I am experiencing an inner life that I had never had before and it seems to grow with each passing day. Often during the day, I will say in my mind, "Lord God of the universe and of my being, I love You and I love myself. I thank You for my sobriety, my serenity, my sanity, and my spirituality." And finally, to quote Dr. Wayne Dier, I truly believe there is no way to happiness; happiness *is* the way. And living in recovery has given me this reward. The Kingdom of Heaven is truly within.

14

A Nurse's Story

Many people wish to shed excess weight, and many people believe that medical science can provide a chemical that will enable them to do this rapidly and easily. Diet pills are just one of the many ways in which vulnerable people may develop an addictive illness. The following account by a nurse illustrates this as well as the phenomenon of multiple addiction. It demonstrates how alcoholism and/ or drug addiction and their sequelae can present clinically as a mental disorder, defying correct diagnosis even by competent psychiatrists.

Case 15: Up and Down with Chemicals

Hi, my name is Agnes, and I am an alcoholic. I remember when that was impossible for me to say, and I fought it tooth and nail. I was diagnosed as psychotic and that I could accept. Crazy, yes; alcoholic, no. but today I can say I am an alcoholic and a grateful alcoholic, too.

I'm a nurse and I worked today from 7 to 3. I put in a full day's work and had a good day. I have a nice home where I prepared dinner tonight for my husband and two children. They appear to be happy with me as their wife and mother. Thank God that's the way it is now, but that's not the way it always was.

I never planned to be an alcoholic and I don't think I inherited it, because neither of my parents was alcoholic. In fact, my own addiction didn't even begin with alcohol. When I graduated from nurses' training, I don't think I had ever drunk anything to speak of. There was just no need to; I didn't like the stuff and could never understand why anyone else did. But I was a little too heavy in my last year of nursing school and I wanted to lose weight, so I asked one of the doctors in the hospital for some pills to help me. Sure, I knew I could lose weight by watching how much I ate and by doing appropriate exercises, but that meant effort, and I saw no reason to expend effort on something that could be accomplished more easily with the help of a pill. This doctor was very compassionate, as many doctors are, especially to a young nurse who needs help, and he gave me a prescription for diet pills. Well, the diet pills did help my appetite, but they also did a lot more for me. I never was the most energetic person on earth. I made it through the day and did what had to be done all right, but it took effort. There is that word again: effort. I guess I felt that it was some kind of obscene word, or maybe I was just born with an allergy to effort. At any rate, I never did see any sense in making an effort unless it was absolutely unavoidable.

Taking the diet pills opened my eyes to a whole new world! I no longer had to exert myself to get through the day. I did things with an ease and speed and comfort that I had never known before. This was the real me! Except that after about four or five hours the "real me" began to vanish and that other person came along who had to be pushed to do everything. But of course, I found that I could get the "real me" back with another pill and things were just fine.

I graduated and went to work and I performed well. Now I can't remember just when I found that it took more than one pill to bring out my "true" personality, but it wasn't long before I was taking five or six pills a day and zipping along just fine. Meanwhile, I had been dating the man I'm married to now. After we got married, he was working and so was I, and he didn't think anything was wrong. My performance at work was really good and the supervisor knew she could always count on me because I never said no. If they needed a nurse to take care of two units because someone else had called in sick, they knew they could count on me. With another little pep pill, I could take care of two units easily, and I did! In fact, with enough pills I bet I would have had the energy to take care of the whole hospital. Double shift? Sure! No problem. They never had any cause for worry as long as I was around, and I felt I was appreciated. That was very important to me.

In those days, there never was much of a problem in getting all the pills you needed. It's not like today where you have to play games with different doctors. I would simply tell the druggist that I needed a refill, and he'd give me a refill of 200 pills without as much as batting an eyelash. After a while, something did happen though. You see I was coming home, jumping around the house like a jack rabbit, and I was so fired up that I couldn't get to sleep. I mean that at one o'clock in the morning I was still zipping around the house. We didn't have any children then and I guess I was looking for things to do. I used to iron my husband's socks. I think he thought this was strange but must have written it off to my trying to be a super-efficient wife. Anyway, I just couldn't settle down, so my husband suggested that maybe a glass of wine at dinner would help and it did. But it didn't help quite enough, so I took another glass after dinner, then another to help me sleep.

Now, I don't know about you people, but my system seems to ascribe to the "all or nothing" law, at least when it comes to chemicals. I needed more and more wine to bring me down, until my husband began to think I was drinking too much. There was no way I could get along with less wine, and when I noticed my drinking was upsetting him, I did the only logical thing, which was to hide the bottles. Our house had tall hedges around it and instead of bringing the bottles into the house, I used to hide them in the bushes and then go out whenever I needed a drink. My husband began to question why I was always running out of the house so late at night so I told him that the house was stuffy and I needed the fresh air. But what to do with all the empties? I didn't want them to accumulate visibly in the garbage cans, so I used to bag them and drop them off in the Goodwill bin a couple of blocks from our home.

This state of affairs continued until one day for no apparent reason, the druggist who used to refill my original prescription suddenly refused. "Agnes," he said "you've been getting this prescription filled now for over five years, and I'm not going to give you any more without another doctor's prescription." I thought the man had gone insane. Here I'd been getting 200 pills about every three weeks, and now he was going to cut me off without any sensible reason! But no amount of arguing helped. No prescription, no pills.

Well, I called the doctor who had given me the original prescription and he told me the druggist had called and told him I was getting about 300 pills a month. The doctor was appalled. He told me I was taking far too many pills and he would not renew the prescription unless I first underwent a complete examination. However, he was leaving town the next day, and the first appointment I could get would be about ten days later.

Maybe if my head hadn't been so muddled, I would have thought of some way to get a temporary supply. Instead, I turned to the only other support I had and got out the wine bottle during the day as well as at night. A few days later (I don't remember this part clearly), my husband says that I became a zombie and just sat and stared. I wouldn't respond to him or anyone or anything. He didn't know what to do with me, and I ended up for the first of many visits in a psychiatric hospital, where I stayed for three weeks or so. I don't remember too much about that period of time, but when I left I was given pills for depression and pills for sleep. That's what I was: depressed. I was not to go back to work until I was ready.

For some reason, I didn't resume drinking right away. I sat around the house, did as little as I could get away with, and got pregnant. My mother came and helped for a while. Later, when the baby was about 2 years old, I felt it was time to get back to work. But by this time, I found I was heavy again, never having lost the weight I'd gained during the pregnancy, and again I told the doctor I needed something to lose weight. He gave me more diet pills but just one a day, and when the prescription ran out three weeks before it was supposed to, he refused to give me any more. But this time I was smarter. I called the druggist and told him that I was the doctor's nurse and that it was okay to refill the prescription. I also found out that several other women in the neighborhood were getting diet pills from their doctors and that helped. I went to these doctors, and soon I was getting prescriptions from three different doctors and having them filled in different drugstores. Sometimes I gave the druggist the names of other women who I knew were getting diet pills and I picked up their prescriptions, too.

Of course, I had to go back to wine to bring me down at night, but now I also had sleeping pills to help me come down, and one day I awoke in the hospital. I knew I hadn't tried to kill myself, but I guess the mixture of wine and pills had been too much, and it looked as though I had attempted suicide. I did get very depressed while in the hospital. You see, I didn't know that when you came off diet pills, you can go into a deep depression or as they call it, "crashing." I hadn't told the doctor I was taking these pills and to make a long story short, I was given shock treatment for the depression. They said I was better and sent me home with more pills for my nerves and pills for sleep. Well, the same scenario repeated itself, actually four times in three years, and I guess the psychiatrist just got sick and tired of the repetition, so he sent me to a state hospital. He told me and my husband that I was incurable. In the meantime, we'd had our second child, and I had acquired a new disease. This time I was supposed to be suffering from post-partum depression. But no one ever said I was drinking too much or taking too many pills.

I don't have any pleasant memories of the state hospital. You can't really, you know, but I am grateful for one thing. There they treated me with benign neglect, which was just what I needed. No pills, no shock, no nothing. I got up in the morning, went to my job assignment in the cannery, and kept my mouth shut. I didn't bother the doctors and they didn't bother me. After a couple of months I was permitted to spend weekends at home, and my head began to clear up. I made friends with one of the nurses there and as I became more human again, I found her to be a good companion. She told me I had been drinking too much and that I ought to go to the AA meetings that were held twice a week in the hospital. I didn't see any reason why I should go, because, of course, I wasn't an alcoholic, but there was nothing better to do, so I went. I thought the stories I heard were pretty funny, since, of course, they didn't in any way relate to me.

I stayed in the state hospital for seven months and when I was discharged they said that too much idle time would lead to more depression, so I went into private duty nursing. It wasn't too long before it was discovered that I was getting more pills than my patients, and I was nailed. But this time nobody said I was crazy. Someone said I was drug addicted and instead of sending me to a psychiatric hospital, they sent me to a rehabilitation center for four weeks. Now you might remember that I said that I could accept being crazy much easier than being alcoholic. In retrospect, I think the reason for this was that if I was crazy, then it was the doctor's job to find the medicine or treatment that was going to make me better, and the burden was on him. However, if I was alcoholic, there was really not much that he could do, and it was my job to get well. Being crazy has its advantages, because you are not the one who has to do the work. Well, I went to this rehabilitation place and this time there were no pills and no treatments, just a constant emphasis on the fact that my life had become uncontrollable because of alcohol and pills, and that as long as I avoided these I had a chance of doing well, but that if I ever went back to them they would drive me further and further into insanity.

Next week will be nine years that I came back from the rehabilitation center, and I have been coming back to this AA program ever since. It didn't all happen that easily, but I am back at work. I can tell you truthfully that I am not depressed and I am not psychotic. I have enough energy to do the housework even after a full day's work, and I don't need any pills to get me through the day, nor any booze to get me through the night. I had spent many months in mental hospitals, and I received treatments I may not have needed. I don't blame anyone. It was I who took the pills, it was I who drank the booze, and it was I who lied about it. But I know now that I don't have to blame myself either, anymore. I have a disease called alcoholism, which I really didn't ask for, and which I'll never get rid of. But with the help of this program, I have that disease under control. I now have a choice whether to take the pills or drink or not. Once upon a time, I didn't have that choice, because the disease was bigger than I was. But today I have your help, and we are bigger than the disease.

I see some of the younger nurses taking pills for weight and Fiorinal for migraines, Percodan for backaches, and Valium for nerves, and I know that a lot of them are overdoing it just as I did. I try to talk to some of them, often with no result. I can't blame them, because I remember what I was like. My very life depended on those pills and I wouldn't have listened to anyone who tried to take them away from me. It is unfortunate that no one even tried. I wish I could get doctors to realize that those pills are dangerous when they fall into the hands of people like me and that there are many people like me around. I wish I could get psychiatrists to check carefully into the drug and drinking habits of their patients and not take the patient's word as the truth. I see many patients in the hospital now who are lying to their doctors about their pills and their drinking just as I did.

I've watched some of the games nurses play to get drugs. They order twelve vials of Demerol from the pharmacy, and say that there was an error and that the pharmacy only sent up six. I see them order extra pills because the patient spat out the pills. I see them sweet-talking doctors to give them a prescription because they don't have time to go to their own physicians. We nurses are in a high risk profession as far as addiction is concerned. But as for me, my own life is together again and the rewards of being sober are many. My children have a mother and my husband has a wife. I don't do double duty anymore, but I believe that my hospital has a capable nurse in me. My husband and children were in the audience last week when I received my pin for five years' service to the hospital. That pin means a great deal to me. Five years of uninterrupted sanity and productivity. I am the one who wears the pin, but I truthfully say that it is yours every bit as much as mine. I am grateful to all the people in this program for their help. God bless all of you.

15

The Defense Rests:
The Prosecution Never Does
(A View from the Penitentiary)

While virtually every case of chemical dependency involves some degree of denial, rationalization, insidious onset, surreptitious progression, and destructive consequences, rarely are they all present to so striking a degree as in the case of a young attorney whose career was decimated by alcohol and cocaine. After spending several years in a federal penitentiary, he reflcts on what brought him to this state.

Case 16: Handcuffing the D.A.

Looking through the small double window of the plane, I could see my reflection against the vast darkness outside as we began our descent to El Reno Federal Penitentiary, Oklahoma. My mind wandered back a couple of years to the day I had been arrested in the judge's chambers by two FBI agents.

It had been my first homicide case as a defense counsel and I had just delivered my opening remarks to the jury on reasonable doubt, fairness, burden of proof, and the importance of keeping an open mind. The first witness, a pathologist, was called by the Commonwealth, and I had just begun my cross examination. The tipstaff leaned over to the judge and whispered something in his ear. He looked startled, took a short recess, returned from his chambers, adjourned the trial, and asked me to please step into his chambers. There two FBI agents waited with handcuffs and a warrant. "You are under arrest." Not only had I been found to be using cocaine, but while under its crazy effects, I had been involved with some distributors. I, an assistant district attorney, was arrested for being a pusher! Although I was aware of what had happened, I was nevertheless paralyzed with confusion.

My mind shifted back to the present as I looked around and took note of the other passengers and my surroundings. The plane was stripped of all signs of life one would ordinarily expect to find. Instead, gloom permeated the entire cabin. It was dark, quiet, and intimidating. Except for a few federal marshals and the pilot, everyone was a federal prisoner. We were all clad in prison garb and shackled at the wrists and ankles. To further restrict movement, a reinforcing chain was passed through an opening at our extremities connecting itself at our waists. Like everyone else, I was tired, hungry, depressed, and scared. I missed my family and friends. I was the first assistant district attorney in the county ever to be indicted, and now I was facing ten years in federal custody for my involvement with drugs and alcohol. I am writing to share my story with the hope that someone out there may be spared the consequences I now face because I failed to take heed of the early warning signs of addiction and alcoholism.

Alcoholism is a disease: cunning, baffling, and powerful. And what can be said of alcoholism is also true of drug addiction. They are both diseases, both progressive in nature, and once present they lead to indescribable pain and destruction. They spare no one, cross all socioeconomic lines, and have as their victims persons with low self-esteem and well-guarded feelings of inadequacy. That's how it usually starts; that's how it started for me.

In the beginning, drugs and alcohol seemed harmless. As a typical teenager from a low-income environment, I saw that drugs and alcohol were not all that uncommon. I experimented, usually on weekends, making sure to be discreet about my usage, but openly with my peers hoping to gain acceptance from them. Initially, I was concerned about being caught, especially the consequences that I would face at home, but these misgivings had little effect on me when I measured them against the benefits of group acceptance. I continued to experiment with drugs through my teens (especially marijuana), through high school, and after graduation. Though I continued to use drugs with some regularity, the times largely were situational, usually in response to peer pressure at a social gathering. My primary focus was on maintaining a steady relationship with a local girl and working at odd jobs to earn enough money for college. Drugs at this point played a very small role in my life even though they were out there in abundance.

As I matured I was slowly introduced to the adult world of responsibility and tragedy. College was just beginning but already the financial strain of high tuition was starting to mount. There were also pressures at home with my father falling hopelessly into depression over recent business failures. The pressure became overwhelming for him and he took his life in a sudden and violent suicide. The grief, shame, abandonment, anger, and humiliation were indescribable, and to this day I suffer with the lingering scars and memories of that tragedy. My response to this pain as well as to the profound confusion I felt was to seek relief through sedatives. The drugs eased the pain and set up a pattern that I would continue to follow until I came to prison. With this tragedy, and the other pressures mounting, I fell right back to the thinking I used as a teenager. When stress arose, I would escape with drugs. It was simple, quick, and easy. Intoxicated, I thought that I could

work through the issues gracefully, and crawl out of the shell of
isolation that I had started to build around myself. Drugs and
alcohol became my conditional response to stress. It was the way I
chose to move through the world; it was an easy pattern of coping
and one that worked at least in the beginning. I did not realize that
the subtle forms of alcoholic and addictive thinking had firmly
taken root in my psyche, preparing me for the predisposition toward chemical dependency that would later take complete control of my life.

Different theories have been advanced by various researchers
working on the cases of alcoholism. Some leaders in the field
argue that alcoholism and addiction are genetically based, predis-
posing us to the disease at birth. Other notables in the field, such
as Charles Lieber and Marc Schuckit, have concluded from their
studies that addiction to alcohol can, in part, be traced back to a
liver enzyme malfunction. While I think these scientific explana-
tions are significant, and represent important developments in the
field of alcoholism, for the layman, or even the lawyer yearning to
understand more about the disease, they have very little practical
value. Alcoholism is a retrospective disease manifesting its presence only after it is firmly in place, and only after it has caused tremendous damage and upheaval not only to the alcoholic but to his
or her family and profession as well. Divorces occur, careers are
lost, and families are broken, leaving the alcoholic alone and
depressed. Learning that the disease is genetically based, or envi-
ronmentally induced at this point means little to the alcoholic who
is on the brink of emotional and financial bankruptcy—or worse
yet, sitting like me in a prison, divorced and facing Supreme Court
discipline.

After completing my undergraduate studies at Youngstown
State University, I married and moved to Pittsburgh to start my
first year of law school at Duquesne University. My life was going
well and I was proud to be accepted into such a time-honored and
prestigious profession. As is the case for most of us who look back

on our beginnings in law school, my first year was fraught with fear and uncertainty. It was clear that we all felt a sense of desperation, some more honest about it than others, but we managed to find strength as a group. Accordingly, study groups sprang up, friendships formed, and we managed a level of comfort by helping each other. As a group, we worked hard together and drank together, especially on weekends—a perfect time to discuss assignments, critique professors, and plan for the future. The drinking was usually increased around mid-terms and final exams, with myself and a few others relying on Valium and other sedatives to last through the night. Sleep is critical to the law student, especially around exam time, and sedatives and alcohol usually guaranteed that. This reliance on drugs and alcohol seemed popular and harmless. It's obvious to me now that this mode of thinking permeates our profession and promotes widespread drinking and drug abuse.

I survived my first year of law school and for the first time in my life, I felt like I belonged. Unlike the others, however, I had a substantial number of tragedies to deal with. That year my cousin and brother-in-law imitated my father's sudden and violent suicide. I was overwhelmed with grief, barely able to stay in focus, and relied more heavily than ever on chemicals to soothe the pain. I chose not to share my feelings with my colleagues, thinking that I might alienate them. It was our first year, everyone had his own problems to bear and these properly belonged to me. Rather than seek professional help, I chose the form of therapy I was most familiar with—the one that worked in the past when things seemed unmanageable—drugs and alcohol. Not surprisingly, these were easily accessible. Suppliers became my friends. Either they had what I wanted personally, or they knew who did.

As law students, we were all very discreet, taking every precaution to avoid exposure. We worked too hard to lose our standing over a few pills, a small amount of marijuana, or some cocaine. Of course, none of us had a "problem" in the clinical sense. We had everything under complete control, or at least I was certain that I

did. We were the next generation of professionals, armed with a
license to work in law, government, and business. We were being
trained to occupy positions that would enable us to shape policy
and influence the way people conducted their lives. Alcoholism or
addiction were labels that applied to others; not to us. We were
lawyers. This is exactly the inflated sense of self-worth I had while
moving through law school. And it was precisely then that I was
losing myself to cocaine addiction.

My third year came, my marriage fell apart, and there was little
I could do to free myself from the compulsion to use cocaine and
alcohol. When I wasn't using cocaine, I tried other forms of escape
through sedatives, usually Valium or Percoset. I always tried to
have some around to soothe the extremely excitable mood swings
I sometimes experienced from cocaine. Miraculously, I graduated
from law school, separated from my wife, increased my usage, and
somehow managed to pass the bar examination. My life was a complete mess and I honestly had no clue as to why. I had suspicions
that it may have been my drug use, but some of my colleagues were
living the same way, and they hadn't lost their families. I thought
that perhaps part of the problem was my wife. Eventually we
divorced, but not before I began working with a small medical malpractice defense firm. Of course, I was still using cocaine at this
point, but my bouts were periodic, usually occurring on weekends,
giving me enough time to recover for Monday morning at the
office. The firm was relying on insurance companies for the bulk
of its business. Well-placed claim adjusters in the insurance companies decided which firms got their business, so it was important
to entertain them as much as possible. Accordingly, social drinking was encouraged. This lifestyle fit in quite nicely with my need
to drink and use drugs. I took full advantage of the challenge to
keep the claim adjusters happy. Drinking made me somewhat
sluggish, so I used cocaine to counterbalance the lethargy—and
there began one of the sickest and most insane cycles of drug abuse
I could ever imagine. My efficiency level at work started to flag.

My files weren't up to date, I was behind in many of my pleadings, and I found myself frequently requesting extensions and continuances. Strangely, no one seemed to notice because the other defense attorneys representing co-defendants in the case were doing the same thing. I was sluggish at depositions, usually riding on the coattails of the others present, sometimes arriving completely unprepared. Fortunately, this negligence had little effect on the outcome of the case because the senior lawyers in the firm took over the file after I had worked it through the preliminary stages. Suffice it to say that had I stayed with the firm and gained enough seniority to finish a file through to the end, serious complications would have arisen. That didn't happen—I was let go long before that took place. My employment with the firm ended abruptly one day when I arrived a *week* late for work. Apparently, I called in sick one day from a hangover and didn't return until a week later. I say apparently, because I honestly don't remember what happened. I apologized to my boss and left. I was desperately in need of cocaine. Within hours, I was using it again.

With what little money I had saved from working, I continued in this pattern of substance abuse until early 1985. I was unemployed, divorced, and riding the emotional roller coaster of cocaine addiction until one day I finally decided that I'd had enough. I was living in a third floor-attic apartment with no furnishings except for a bed, desk, lamp, a broken table, a few chairs, and a television set. I was lonely, depressed, and thirty to forty pounds underweight. It had gotten so bad I was drinking the grain alcohol left over from the night before. I used grain alcohol because it produced a much cleaner flame for the cocaine than other accelerants. Finally, I called home and told my mother I needed a place to stay to put my life back together and start over. She agreed and I moved home.

It never occurred to me to reach out to my profession for help, but if I had, I wonder what could have been done. In my mind, there was no place to go; I was caught in this fatal downward spiral. I wonder how many other lawyers have felt the same way. I don't know if it is arrogance or apathy that has brought us to the point where we are years behind in the fight against drug and alcohol abuse within the ranks of our profession. Lawyers write the law in our capitals, legislate them in our districts, enforce them in our courts, and shape the way people live at all levels of democracy. We advise heads of state and heads of corporations, and influence business transactions in our cities, at our borders, and abroad. Lawyers write the laws that attempt to redistribute wealth, feed the hungry, clothe the poor, and provide shelter for the homeless. We write the laws that protect the unborn, the newborn, and the helpless. Yet, at that time, not one lawyers' group had established an assistance program in Allegheny County to help the alcoholic or addict lawyer better understand his problem. It is a terrible commentary on how we choose to define ourselves.

Without the help of AA, NA, or an assistance program, I managed to wean myself off cocaine, but had little success with alcohol and sedatives. With cocaine out of my life, or at least for the most part, things seemed somewhat more manageable. I still drank and took sedatives, but not like I had when I was using cocaine. I regained some sense of self-respect and responsibility and decided I was ready to try practicing law again. I was hired at the district attorney's office and moved out of my old home. I was somewhat concerned about my compulsion to use chemicals, especially in the sensitive area of law enforcement. Still, I thought that once I started working, things would change. I had never heard of the concept of cross-addiction and believed that now that I had overcome my cocaine problem, I would be safe from the debilitating effects of substance abuse even if I had a few drinks after work or at a party. I was never more wrong about anything in my life.

Cross-addiction is a simple concept. A person addicted to one drug cannot take any chemical safely again. Once the disease of alcoholism is present, the addiction is not only to alcohol but to all drugs as well. Similarly, once the disease of addiction is present with cocaine, it is present in all other chemicals including alcohol—a simple concept, not widely known—at least not by me when I began my job as an assistant district attorney.

In the beginning, the job was simple. I went through a brief training and orientation period getting acquainted with staff and the supervisors of the various units within the office. Units were broken down according to the severity of crimes. Homicide was the most serious unit and General Trial was where I would begin. After orientation, I was given trainee status where I worked with other more experienced assistants to learn trial strategy and courtroom demeanor. It was all very exciting and most of the others in the office were quick to invite me out after work for a few drinks, to help facilitate my integration into their circles. Drinking seemed as natural a part of office life as it had when I was a law student, and not unlike the experience I had with my previous law firm.

The drinking wasn't quite as regular because I had my appearance to maintain, but it was every bit a part of life as any other job. Shortly after my training, I was assigned a caseload that I was responsible for with much left to my own judgment. As my caseload increased, so did the stress, and before long I was back into the old familiar pattern of dealing with stress the only way I knew—alcohol. I wasn't alone and found it easy to find a colleague to accompany me to a bar after work. After a while, I began to notice that my drinking took on a somewhat different character than it once had. When I drank before, at least at the social level, I would usually stop early in the evening. But now, I noticed I had to have more than the others, and my drinking continued until later in the evening, sometimes past midnight. Months went by and the pattern continued more aggressively, and the next thing I knew, it was beginning to affect my work. I was waking up later in the morning, rushing to work, making it just under the wire, feeling hungover, foggy, and tired. As I gained more seniority in the office, I was given more files, more responsibility, and more difficult cases to manage. I was always feeling overwhelmed, tired, and overworked. Predictably, I started to drink more because my tolerance level to alcohol had increased, only compounding the problems caused by drinking. This is exactly the cycle that Dr. Abraham Twerski outlines in his books. I seemed to need more and more to reach the same effect I had achieved only a month earlier. Little did I know that I had crossed over from cocaine addiction to alcoholism in less than a year. What could be said of my behavior regarding cocaine was now true of alcohol. That's the way it is with cross-addiction. I was right back into the same old cycle.

I started mixing alcohol with prescription pain killers, and soon I started to develop health problems. My life, once again, was out of control, but this time I couldn't identify the problem. As strange as it may sound, I had never associated the unmanageability of my life with the usage of alcohol and prescription drugs.

The cycle continued into a slow but steady form of deterioration, both mental and physical. I was feeling increasingly more fatigued during the day. I was missing work more frequently but being careful not to use up more sick days than I was allotted. I was still performing at the level expected, but I lost my enthusiasm for the job. This, of course, was reflected in my mood, manner, and attitude, but surprisingly few of my colleagues seemed to notice. I am amazed at how little people pay attention to each other in a professional setting where team effort is the only chance of continued success.

I had been with the district attorney's office just under one year and during that time, I had gone from an enthusiastic assistant to an overwrought, uninterested employee, coasting through my job and caring little about my prospects for advancement. The signs of chemical abuse were evident, but went unnoticed. This phenomenon represents another example of how little we know about alcoholism and its early warning signs. One solution might be to promote more seminars dedicated to the subject of alcoholism and to encourage attendance from representatives of each law firm. Steps must be taken to reduce the number of casualties in the war against chemical abuse, not only among ourselves but among our clients as well. Chemical abuse within our ranks, if left unchecked, will continue to progress, further blemishing a profession already in question by many of the population who employ us.

With these problems and others, my career at the district attorney's office was short-lived. I resigned under a shadow of suspicion, fostered in part by a widening federal grand jury probe that would later include me and change my life.

Despite my erratic performance in that office, it didn't take me long to find employment within the defense bar. I had more than one offer, but wound up accepting a position with a small firm whose practice focused primarily on criminal defense. It was the logical choice, given my familiarity with the system. I performed well, brought in new clients, and kept drinking. I married my second wife, and things were going well again. Shortly afterwards, I was offered another position with a different firm that promised more money and more opportunity for advancement. I readily accepted. With my new position, I took on far more responsibility than I'd had with my previous firm and the stress began to mount with each week. The caseload was endless, and although my clients were part of the criminal court system, a specialty I was comfortable with, I was simply on overload. Daily, I was handling magistrate hearings, guilty pleas, non-jury trials, and jury trials that sometimes grew out of a ruptured plea agreement. It was not uncommon for me to handle as many as five or six criminal cases a day with a case or two in the family division that always required more time and research. I felt completely overwhelmed at the end of the day and I began to drink even more heavily. Alcohol was always available, so that was the drug I reached for most frequently. I stepped up my prescription medication again so that in the evenings I was mixing drugs and alcohol. I had activated the cycle all over again, but this time my chemical abuse was at an all time high. I was drinking between ¼ and ½ of a fifth of whiskey almost every evening and mixing that with Darvoset and

Valium to help things along. I was hiding pills and alcohol from my family and waking up in the middle of the night to find relief in the same pattern. My performance at work started to decline, and finally I was calling off work again. I had reached a crisis level in my firm and on more than one occasion I was questioned about my conduct. My security at the firm was being threatened, my marriage was beginning to feel the strain, and I had no idea how to control my drinking. My physical health was deteriorating, and at times I felt like an empty shell running on force of habit. I knew that I couldn't continue much longer in this pattern and some days I felt as though I would simply collapse in the middle of Grant Street from sheer exhaustion, fatigue, and stress. I could sense that my days at the firm were numbered, but still I found it next to impossible to stop using drugs. The issue of what to do became moot when I was indicted.

With my arrest my personal world completely collapsed, and all that was important to me was now in danger of being extinguished. The news media were relentless in their coverage, headlining my story in the press and on television. What seemed like a crisis only a day before paled in comparison to the new and very real crisis that was unfolding. The shock and embarrassment I caused not only to myself but to my family were paralyzing. After that wore off, I tried to reorganize my thinking to somehow place this nightmare in perspective. It was hopeless. The more I thought about it the worse things got, and I continued to drink. I started to withdraw from work and eventually built a protective wall around myself to hide from what was happening. I stayed home as much as possible to close out the world I no longer felt a part of. With this newfound time on my hands, I drank more than ever, practically around the clock, even after I had to seek treatment for liver damage. The specialist whose treatment I sought advised that I "cut back" on the alcohol, apparently unable to diagnose the symptoms of an alcoholic completely out of control. Still I continued to drink. Nothing was working. I was profoundly unhappy, falling faster than ever into a dark sense of hopelessness.

It was at this time that a colleague of mine who was following my case in the newspapers, phoned to offer support and concern. She repeatedly urged me to seek drug and alcohol treatment and even dragged me to my first AA meeting. She was relentless in her attempt to stop my self-destruction. It took awhile, but finally I gave in. I checked into Gateway Rehabilitation Center, making one of the most important decisions in my life. Through its counselors and staff, Gateway brought my life into focus, placing before me everything I needed to learn about myself and my condition. This knowledge had little effect on the outcome of my sentencing, but it helped me take my life back in a way that has given me a tremendous sense of relief and freedom. Freedom, I have learned, is largely a mindset not always controlled by things outside the self. Much of it has to do with one's perspective and personal levels of peace and tranquility. I no longer respond to outside forms of stress the way I used to. Alcohol and drugs no longer control my thinking, my emotions, my motives, or my plans. For these reasons I'm much freer today than I was on the outside, even though I share this story from a federal camp in Duluth, Minnesota. In many ways, I consider myself fortunate. If I hadn't been indicted and urged into treatment, I would still be out there drinking myself into aimlessness or self-destruction. Today my life is different from what it used to be; today there is hope.

Since the writing of this story, the lawyer completed his sentence and entered a halfway house, which provides extended treatment for addicts. He eventually applied for reinstatement to practice law and it was granted, subject to monitoring. At the time of this writing he is again working in his chosen profession and providing a helpful service to peers who enter recovery. He is also active in addressing young people to acquaint them with the treachery of alcohol and drug abuse with the hope of preventing them from following the destructive course he had taken.

16

Another High Bottom Miracle

Denial, which is present in virtually 100 percent of cases of alcoholism, is generally not overcome until some event occurs that shocks the alcoholic into facing the reality of his condition. This phenomenon is referred to as "hitting a rock bottom." Sometimes the rock bottom is a cataclysmic event that takes a physical or emotional toll. If one is fortunate, a relatively minor event may suffice to break through the denial and initiate recovery. We refer to the former as a "low bottom" and to the latter as a "high bottom." One recovering alcoholic phrased it well. "Alcoholism is an elevator going down. You can get off on any floor, or wait until the cable breaks and you plummet to the bottom of the shaft." Jennifer was fortunate in having a "high bottom."

Case 17: Jennifer

If you think you've still got time to drink because you've not yet wrecked a car, gotten a DUI, lost a job, lost a family, or lived in a gutter, keep reading. I never did any of those things, but I am an alcoholic. I am also a woman.

My story is a "high bottom" one—I was lucky enough to find AA before I wrecked any cars, received any DUIs, lost my family, or experienced any of the other things frequently equated with the conclusion that someone is an alcoholic. There is no doubt in my mind that I am an alcoholic and that I hit bottom before I came to AA. However, my bottom wasn't a street gutter—it was an emotional gutter.

My father was an alcoholic and all of his children were afraid of him. I can remember spending a lot of time hoping he would either come right home after work or come home at least three hours late. Anything in between meant that he would verbally abuse my mother and terrify the kids. If he came home three hours late, he would be so drunk he couldn't talk, much less yell, so that all we had to do was untie his work boots and lead him to bed. As a consequence, bringing friends home was out of the question, so I was pretty much of a loner. Life with Daddy was chaotic so my siblings and I became "model" children. I can never remember being disciplined for anything. We simply did not step out of line. I was an overachiever in school and buried myself in my school work.

As a result, I vowed never to become like my father. With my first drink, I blacked out and had to be taken home. Later, after coming to AA, I learned that blackouts are one of the telltale signs of an alcoholic. I put myself through college and law school, all the while trying to maintain the "good girl" image, but inside I was a mess. I was a chronic people-pleaser because the thought that someone might not like me was too hard to bear. I always felt "less than" and was constantly criticizing others in order to make myself look good. I resented everyone and everything. I always had at least two or three boyfriends at the same time—to feed my ego—yet all of these relationships were dishonest because I never told any of them that I was also dating others, and of course I demanded that each of them see only me. I had many friends—people I would have done anything for—yet I was completely alone because I never opened up to anyone or ever asked for help for myself. Toward the end of my drinking, I was also very fearful and paranoid. I was afraid I would die in a car accident; I worried about family members dying in an accident; I worried that people were talking about me; I felt like something "bad" was going to happen at any moment. My fears would overcome me and I could not sleep, yet on the outside I was "little miss wonderful" to the rest of the world.

My only relief from all the panic and terror I felt inside came from drinking. I was never a daily drinker but when I drank, I could not guarantee that I would only have one or two. I can remember sharing with one friend that we just couldn't drink anymore, because neither of us could handle booze. Four or five drinks and I would be bombed. I'd black out and end up in a strange bed or make a fool of myself in a bar. The next day, I'd call up friends and ask what I had done and whether I had offended anyone. I drank fast, and became annoyed at other women who would order "pansy" drinks or nurse the same drink all night.

In my overachiever ways, I worked, went to school, and somewhere in there, married and had children. My life was full, and in the last few years before I came to AA, my drinking was at its lowest point. But whenever my husband was out of town or there was a social function that "entitled" me to drink, I was off and running. All the while though, this overwhelming sense of impending doom and fear of death were paralyzing me. Being a lawyer made it even worse because of all the pressure of having to be the best at whatever I did. I was a nervous wreck and I did not know why. I *never* thought it was alcoholism because in comparison with my father's drinking, I was a lightweight.

A friend of mine came into AA and started telling me about it. I got the brilliant idea that it would be good for my father, and after he fell off the wagon following a one-year dry spell, I went to an AA meeting to investigate. The woman who spoke was nothing like me. She was unemployed and seemed to be a "loser"—not like me—"Miss Law Review, Miss Successful Lawyer, Wife, Mother, Daughter, and Friend." Suddenly it dawned on me that she was the "winner" and I was the "loser." I was a fraud—a model citizen on the outside and a complete mess on the inside. I identified with her feelings and with everything she said. I started to cry because I knew that I belonged there. I stayed, not for my father, but for myself, and I've been in AA ever since. I now know that my blackouts, my chronic people-pleasing, my low self-esteem, my sense of impending doom, and my irrational fears are all common characteristics of the disease of alcoholism. I also know that you don't have to sleep in gutters or wreck cars to get here.

I'm not a phony anymore. I can tell people my feelings, I can stand up for myself, I can talk about things without inspiring resentment, I can believe in myself. My fear of impending doom was miraculously lifted and AA continues to be a miracle every single day.

17

The Flying Nun

An alcoholic nun? You must be kidding.

Nuns are human, too.

Monsignor Honan related that his parish once sponsored a picnic, to which the parishioners brought their little children. In those days nuns wore the full habit, and some of the children who had never seen a nun before were a bit frightened by their rather unusual appearance.

One nun tried to make friends with a child and picked him up. The child began crying and kicking and the nun tried to calm him, speaking softly and petting him. After a few minutes the child stopped crying, sized her up, and with a broad smile turned to his mother. "They is girls!" he announced.

"Yes, they is girls." Of course, our culture has always had a double standard. Whereas excessive drinking among men is frowned upon, it is nevertheless tolerated. "Frank is really a good guy. Just overdoes it a bit. Too much of a good thing." But if Betty gets drunk, horrors! She is obviously a totally immoral, promiscuous woman. Nobody would think of Frank as being a bad father, but

Betty is a disgrace to the family and a failure as a mother. If this is true about women in general, how much more so of devout women, especially a nun.

The alcoholic's denial is often reinforced by those about her who refuse to acknowledge the condition. Husbands cover up for their wives' drinking because of the terrible stigma, and effective treatment is thus delayed, because both husband and wife believe the problem is something other than alcoholism. If a psychiatrist is consulted, the diagnosis is apt to be depression or anxiety disorder, with the excess alcohol consumption being only a symptom of an underlying problem, and the psychiatrist tries to treat this underlying problem. Far be it from him to insult this dignified woman by labeling her alcoholic. He prescribes anti-depressants which are ineffective either because there is no underlying depression, or if there is, the medication is counteracted by the alcohol. He may prescribe tranquilizers for the anxiety and sleeping pills for the insomnia, which results in the patient becoming addicted to both. I recall one nun who had been treated repeatedly for depression, and when all medication failed to relieve it, she received a course of electroshock treatments that were equally futile. Years later, when the existence of alcoholism in religious communities was recognized, this nun admitted having been a closet drinker during all the years she had sought treatment, but never confided in her doctor that she was a heavy drinker.

Sister J. had her first contact with alcohol at age 10. This was before the Council of Vatican II, when the priests would say mass with their backs to the congregation. The wine of the mass was set to one side, then taken to a place called the saquarium, where it was to be disposed of. "We kids did church work, and I polished off that wine," she confided.

Sister J.'s next experience with alcohol did not come until years later, and then only on holidays, the only time when alcohol was served. "I volunteered to clear off the table, so that I could finish whatever wine remained in the glasses." Following the changes by the Council of Vatican II, when nuns were permitted to move about more freely and no longer wore distinctive garb, Sister J. would buy her liquor at the store or drink in bars.

Sister M., on the other hand, never drank. She was a school teacher who was admitted to the hospital because of a convulsion, and when all tests were negative, she was diagnosed as having epilepsy and was prescribed anti-convulsant medication. She was hospitalized several times each year for recurrent convulsions, and the doctors were stymied as to why the anti-convulsant medications were not working. It finally emerged that Sister M. had access to the medicine cabinet in the infirmary and had developed a rather severe addiction to sleeping pills and tranquilizers. The convulsions were withdrawal seizures that occurred when her access to drugs was curtailed.

Nuns can be alcoholic, and nuns can be drug addicted. Let's listen to Sister S.'s account.

Case 18: Alcohol, the Pseudo-Friend

I am writing this to share with you two very important aspects of my life. I am a sister, a Catholic nun, and I am an alcoholic. I used to believe, and many people actually do believe, that these two things can't ever go together in one person. They just don't fit; you must be either one or the other. In the process of recovery, those two aspects of my personality have become integrated and continue to be.

Both my alcoholism and my membership in a religious community were part of a journey. The journey toward religious life passed a significant marker on the road, when in 1979 at the age of 30, I entered a religious community of women. I'm not really sure why I made that decision at that time in my life. But it was always something that attracted me, and for some reason I had the freedom and grace to give it a try. This decision was to move me

650 miles away from my family and friends and that was pretty terrifying. It was like starting all over, yet I knew I had to give it a try. I just knew I'd never be happy if I kept putting off what I had a sense my heart was telling me.

So against all odds, I made the big move from home to another city. Soon I was pretty homesick, missing my family and friends. I began to teach, and would come back and hang around the convent. There was tremendous loneliness much of the time because this was such unfamiliar territory. I hated that empty lonely feeling but felt that in time it would pass as I adjusted. Actually as the year progressed, I found that I really liked the sisters I was living with and found them welcoming and supportive. Yet I was very lonely. This was not in any way their fault, but mine. They tried to get close to me but I would not let them.

The other very important aspect of my personality that I have come to recognize is that I am an alcoholic. I did not know that back in 1979 and 1980. It took a few years for it to become clear to me. For a while, I just chalked it up to adjustment. The years that followed, however, began to suggest that I was in trouble and that trouble had to do with my drinking. Living at home, I could justify my drinking to myself and others. I was in denial that there was a problem. An uncle of mine had died of alcoholism and I was nothing like him. He was dirty, homeless, and would show up every now and then; whenever he appeared, everyone got upset. No, I was nothing like him. I was a pretty heavy drinker in those days and about once or twice a week I got quite drunk, but I was never caught driving drunk and never hurt anyone. I just had a lot of fun and it helped me unwind. I was clean, went to work every day, and was an excellent teacher.

When I moved, all of the people, places, and things changed in my life. It was pretty hard to cope. Here I was in a new city with no friends—it was a lot to adjust to. It was a whole new life style for me, filled with strangers. I needed a best friend, and I found her in alcohol. (Hereafter, I will refer to alcohol as "my friend," because that is what it was. At least I felt at that time that alcohol was my friend, my best friend, and my only friend.) Soon, I had become a daily closet drinker. Some days I drank openly, and on other days I went off alone with my "friend." My "best friend" began to take me away from the sisters because she warned me they would not understand. She was right. Slowly, the drinking became more and more secretive and I did it alone. She also convinced me that I could really relax with her, just like I used to back home. It worked for me then, why wouldn't it work now? She reassured me that I was okay and that this move hadn't been a mistake. She could help me adjust if I just relied on her and slowly her power over me grew.

Sometimes she took me places, but I couldn't remember where the next day. Sometimes I got really mad at her, and didn't want to go when she called, but she always managed to convince me that she was really helping with all of those feelings I had. Only she could really understand me.

After a while she told me to steal money for her, and told me to lie and keep our relationship a secret. I did all of that and just kept getting sicker and sicker. I was able to justify the stealing by telling myself that if these sisters knew so much about life, surely they would drink more and provide alcohol so that I wouldn't be forced to steal. They knew I liked to have a few drinks every now and then. After all I had given up to join this community, the least they could do was keep a supply of beer around. If they did that simple thing, I wouldn't have to go out so much. "My friend" pointed out that if they really liked me so much, they'd do more to help me. So, I relied on her more and more and removed myself from the sisters I lived with.

Most people, when they relate their drinking histories, describe funny things that happened during this period. These things appear funny only in retrospect, but were either dead serious or disasters at the time they happened. I can't think of anything very funny that happened to me, except perhaps this. The only place I could hide in the convent to drink was the basement, but why would I be spending so much time in the basement? Why, to wash clothes, of course. So I had stashed my beer in the basement, where I would wash my clothes, put them in the dryer, take them out of the dryer and put them back in the washer, then in the dryer again, for several cycles. I'm not sure whether I was trying to fool myself or the other sisters, but that's what I did. The only redeeming feature of this craziness was that I had the cleanest clothes in the entire community.

Needless to say, I went downhill fast. It was becoming apparent that I was in deep trouble. The only thing I could do was be honest and tell the sister in charge. I really wanted to do what was right; the lying and stealing had become too much for me and I could no longer keep the secret. I didn't really tell her too much of what I was feeling, but I did tell her I thought I was an alcoholic. Much to my surprise, she didn't ask me to leave but suggested I get help. I was so relieved that I began to feel like I had again entered safe territory, that things would be okay again. But what I did not realize was just how powerful "my friend" was. I couldn't beat her alone and things were not okay.

Now that the secret was out she never let up on me. She kept me awake and was always after me. She constantly tricked me and whenever I let my guard down, she came after me and I broke out in a drunk. I hated her and I hated me. I was trapped. If I was alone she took me. I was her prisoner and had no idea how to get free.

Desperate for some kind of peace, I went to see a priest who was a drug and alcohol counselor in a city three hours away. He told me I was sick and talked to me about the disease I had. I felt so ashamed and had no real understanding of what was happening. Once a month, for the next year, I went to see him to try to deal with the alcoholism. But "my friend" was always over my shoulder, telling me not to believe him. She tried to convince me that I was not like those people he talked about; I was stronger. She told me again that she was my "best friend," and that he was just trying to take me away from her.

The priest suggested that I go to AA once a week and I initially tried that, but I couldn't keep it up. After all, people might recognize me there. What an embarrassment to my community! I felt it was better driving three hours to talk to him, and in that way only he and my superior would have to know. "My friend" came with me on every one of those rides, but I drank only on the way home. She helped me figure out what had gone on in the session and reminded me of how I could lie to keep us together.

I soon became frustrated and told my superior that this trip to the priest was helping a little, but sometimes I still had to drink. She, too, suggested AA and again I gave it try. So, for the next year I went to AA meetings once a week. I sat in the back next to the only homeless man there. I focused on him and was able to block out what was being said. I was unaware of the forty or fifty other people in the room. After the meeting, I would buy a six-pack, go to a local park and read the Big Book. I did not understand it; in fact, I hated it. It seemed poorly written and the language was definitely not inclusive. There were a few stories about women, but not one about a nun, so I was sure this book was not for me. I went to the meetings but no magic occurred. I was simply not getting drunk as often. And when I did drink, I'd feel really terrible because I had lost my capacity. It made me sick a lot.

Even though my drinking became very infrequent and months passed between episodes, I still felt trapped. I had no real peace and out of fear, I decided to go into a rehab. I was pretty convinced it wouldn't help a lot, but I was too scared of hiding from "my friend." Maybe there, she wouldn't find me. I had been hiding from her for nine months but knew it was only a matter of time before she found me. I could not hold on for much longer so I went to a rehab.

I was admitted to the rehab as Sister Sue, but they immediately dropped the "Sister" because it was not important. I was just like the rest of the drunks there. I was both insulted and relieved. I listened and I learned. They told me what to do and I did it. I found God; I found friends, and I found a community I had always longed for. I entered the community of AA and it saved my life.

Four years later, I found myself making my final vows before several hundred people. On that day I was able to do what I had learned to do privately each day at the rehab: get on my knees before God and ask for help to make it through this day. And every day since, I am able to take what has become a familiar position before God and offer to Him the life He gave back to me just a few years before.

18

When School Is Over

Resistance to accepting treatment for chemical dependency is unusually high among teachers. Pennsylvania has advocacy and assistance groups for doctors, dentists, nurses, pharmacists, psychologists, and lawyers, but none exists for teachers, whose vulnerability to chemical dependency is no less than other professionals.

Case 19: Parents + Teachers + Students = Alcohol

Lester was clearly not happy with his superintendent's insistence that he consult me about an alcohol problem. Yes, he drank but he had no problem with alcohol, and the incident was being blown out of proportion.

Lester was the principal of a large high school, and felt that he was in the midst of a system that was essentially unworkable. In fact, he deserved a commendation for keeping a hole-ridden ship afloat, rather than a reprimand and being considered an alcoholic.

"He must understand the position I'm in. Everything that can possibly go wrong with the educational system has done so. Kids are wild and unmotivated and many of them are drinking or using marijuana. Scholastic performance is at an all-time low, and the parents, who are not in the least bit helpful in disciplining the kids or demanding that they get serious about school work, place the blame on the school. They give their kids cars and let them have booze parties and expect us to motivate and teach them.

"Teachers are underpaid, constantly threatening to strike, and their morale is poor. Students have no respect for teachers. Teachers gripe to the principal about the deplorable atmosphere in the school. The school board cuts the budget and expects us to work magic. The board is comprised of a group of people who know less than nothing about education, and when they get complaints from parents about their children's poor scholastic achievements, the board dumps on the superintendent who then dumps on me, and I'm caught in the middle of a tug of war.

"After an exhausting and frustrating school day, I have to go through the halls to check on things. Teachers leave the lights on, windows open, and God knows what else. When I leave the building, I stop off for one or two beers, and who wouldn't? It's the only livable half-hour of the day.

"When I get home I try to relax with a newspaper. Sometimes I take another beer. That particular day I had gotten it from all sides, and I had two beers before dinner. Furthermore, I had to anticipate returning to school that evening for an open house where parents meet with teachers, and needless to say, I was not looking forward to it. At the open house, several parents complained about one teacher, and believe me, that teacher is a saint if she stays in this school. These particular kids are behavior problems, and the parents were doing nothing to control them. The parents said some very nasty things about the teacher and it was more than I could take. I guess I lost it and told them where to get off.

"The next day some parents called the school board and said that I smelled of alcohol, and maybe I did. I hadn't eaten dinner that night because my stomach was all in knots anticipating the encounter with griping parents. They said I had shouted obscenities, which was not true. At any rate, this is why I'm here. I think I have a problem, but it's not alcohol. I'm 52 and stuck in an impossible job for at least several more years until I reach retirement age."

Lester claimed to have a good marriage, so I suggested it would be helpful to have his wife come in and share the interview. She did, and said, "I'm glad you asked me to come. Lester asked me not to tell you about his drinking, but for his own good, I must."

His wife's account of Lester's drinking was quite different from his. He often came home late at night quite drunk, having spent four hours rather than half an hour at the bar. Communication between the two had been reduced to zero, and this was also true of Lester's relationship with his children.

We may indeed empathize with Lester's predicament, but this is just another variety of "If you had my job you'd drink too." Many life situations are full of stress, but stress is not the cause of alcoholism. A successful adjustment to life requires coping effectively with stressful situations rather than escaping from them into alcohol or drugs.

Lester entered treatment essentially under protest. He was superficially compliant with the program, but clearly did not accept his inability to control alcohol. After discharge he did not follow through with the aftercare plan and resumed drinking. A bit later he was readmitted following a drunk-driving accident in which his car was totalled. His participation in the relapse program this time was much more sincere, and he has remained sober since. He resigned his position as principal, was able to get an academic position elsewhere, and has been functioning satisfactorily.

Realizing the need for an outreach service to educators and the overwhelming resistance within this group to acknowledging chemical dependency, and in the absence of action by any teacher organization, I personally organized a group of recovering teachers and principals for this purpose. We installed a hotline, distributed thousands of brochures to schools and colleges, explaining that we were a group of recovering educators willing to assist their peers with their chemical dependency problems. It was made clear that there was no affiliation with any official body, and absolute confidentiality was guaranteed. One need only call the hotline and leave a first name and telephone number, and a recovering educator would return the call.

I met with most of the school superintendents in the area and they were supportive of this concept. They said that any teachers who sought help for a chemical dependency problem could rest assured that they would not be jeopardizing their jobs. Yet, we subsequently learned that in some schools the brochures had not been distributed because the official responsible for that school, principal, or other, did not feel that they had a problem.

The hotline was in operation for three years. Many calls came through, but less than one percent of callers left their first name and number. In interviewing some teachers who were admitted for treatment, I asked if they had known about the service and whether they had called the hotline. Some said they had, but were afraid to leave their name and number for fear that someone of officialdom might discover they had a chemical dependency problem.

This apparent paranoia among teachers is not without some justification. Most teachers do trust their superintendents' good intentions in guaranteeing their tenure, but are afraid that if the word gets out that a teacher had an alcohol or drug problem, the parents would put pressure on the school board and superintendent to dismiss the teacher. "We don't want a drunk or junkie teaching our children." Teachers were concerned that their superiors would not be able to withstand the political pressure and they would indeed lose their jobs.

Case 20: Letters from Texas

Elaine was 39, and taught elementary school. She was admitted for treatment of Fiorinal and Percocet addiction. Elaine had developed severe recurrent headaches, and had no relief from aspirin, Tylenol, or ibuprofen. She was prescribed Fiorinal and for severe headaches took Percocet. Over the years the dosage of these medications progressively increased, and she began having memory lapses, mood swings, and uncontrollable crying spells. Her husband correctly suspected that the drugs were causing her emotional problem and she was seen for evaluation.

Elaine agreed that she needed help but was fearful that exposure of her problem would result in her dismissal. She therefore concocted a story that her sister in Texas was very ill, and that she was needed there to help with the children. She received a six-week leave of absence on the basis of hardship and entered treatment. While in treatment she wrote letters to her principal, colleagues, and friends, and sent them to her sister in Texas who would mail them from there, so that they would bear a Texas postmark, in order to corroborate her story.

Elaine has been free of drugs for six years now. The headaches have not recurred. She travels twice a week to another town thirty-five miles away to attend AA and NA. (Although she never drank, Elaine identifies with alcoholics more than with drug addicts and prefers AA to NA.) In spite of her excellent record as a teacher, Elaine is still convinced that had her treatment for chemical dependency six years earlier become known it would have been held against her.

This attitude is quite prevalent among teachers. It is crucial that the educational system adopt a more enlightened position. Until they do so, *active* addicts and alcoholics rather than *recovered* chemically dependent people will be teaching our children. It is of interest that in working with adolescents, I found that the youngsters are well aware of which teachers are chemically dependent. The only ones who do not wish to know are the parents, whose unenlightened attitude results in suppression of the problem, but certainly not in its elimination.

19

All That Ice Cream, Free!
(A Pharmacist's Story)

While there are no accurate statistics about drug addiction among health professionals, it is possible that the combination of stress at work and the easy availability of drugs may increase the incidence of chemical abuse and dependency. Of course, stress may not necessarily be job related. Stress from any source may lead to recourse to chemical relief when drugs are readily available.

Case 21: Daniel

Ever since I was a kid I dreamt of working in a drug store. Our corner drug store had a soda fountain where we would buy ice cream, chocolate sodas, and banana splits. I used to watch the soda jerk make these delicacies, scooping out ice cream from the large containers. I used to think, "Man, how lucky can a guy get! He can have all the ice cream he wants, any flavor, all the time, for free!" The man at the other end of the store who wore a white jacket didn't attract my attention at all. It never would have occurred to me that he, too, had access to a lot of "goodies" for free.

I don't know what psychologists would think, but I doubt that my envy of the soda jerk's unlimited access to ice cream had anything to do with my becoming a pharmacist and working in a drug store. Maybe it did. The human mind, especially the unconscious part of it, is a funny thing.

I have nothing spectacular to relate about my childhood. My parents were loving, stable people. My father was employed as a store manager and my mother worked in a beauty shop. I have one younger sister. We were never rich, but we certainly weren't poor. I can't think of myself as being deprived of anything.

During later high school years and in college we partied. I got drunk a few times, but no big deal. I didn't drink regularly, but I guess I drank at parties so as not to be different. I smoked some pot but never really took to it.

When I was 17, I broke my elbow falling off a bicycle. It was a nasty fracture and required surgery and pinning. I was prescribed Percocet for pain and I liked it. After the fracture healed and the pain subsided, the doctor did not prescribe any more Percocet and I never tried to get any.

I met Kim at a party in my second year of pharmacy school. I wasn't thinking of pharmacy school as a way to get drugs, or at least not consciously. At this time I wasn't drinking or smoking pot to any appreciable degree. Kim got pregnant and we decided to get married.

After graduation I got a job in a drug store, and we had a second child, another daughter, who was born with a cleft palate. Kim and I both took this very hard. Kim's parents never liked me. I guess they didn't like the way we got married. During this same year my father died, and my mother was a very needy person. Kim and I were left without any family support at a time when we were going through a great deal of distress with a baby who required several operations. Instead of being drawn closer by our common burden, Kim and I drifted apart. Kim wanted me home more, and I told her I had to work extra hours because our insurance didn't cover all the medical bills. Kim became very irritable with me and we were always griping at each other.

I must have been vulnerable at this time and developed a romantic relationship with a young woman whom I'd met in college and who now occasionally came into the drug store. Although I felt guilty that I was cheating on Kim, the guilt didn't stop the relationship. Eventually, though, my girlfriend began saying that she didn't want to play second fiddle to anyone, and that if I wasn't intending to get a divorce and marry her, she really wanted to break off. I felt trapped. I couldn't have her but I didn't want to give her up either so I stalled.

It was about this time that I took some Percocet in order to get some sleep. I knew Percocet wasn't a sleeping pill, but I guess I remembered what it had done for me years ago. I wasn't using that many initially, and we were dispensing a good bit of it. If the prescription called for forty, I would dispense thirty-seven and keep three for myself. Few people count their pills. The few that I took out of the stock bottle were not enough to arouse any suspicion.

But then I began needing more. There was one doctor who I knew was selling scripts, so I asked him to write some for me under someone else's name, which he did. Once I must have told my girlfriend what I was doing, although I don't know why.

Our 3 year old was doing well and Kim got pregnant again. I had to make a decision and I told my girlfriend that I could not walk out on Kim, that it would be better if we broke off. She was very hurt by this and retaliated by calling the narcotic agents and telling them about me. At this time I was up to twenty percs a day.

When the narcs confronted me I could have denied the problem, since they really didn't have enough on me to make a case, but I didn't. I broke down and cried and I told them the truth. They were very considerate and told me if I went for treatment they would not press charges.

Kim was really swell about this. Surprisingly, she had never found out about the other relationship. I guess she was naive and trusted me. When my head began to clear, I felt all the worse about what I had done to Kim, since she was now being so supportive. Kim participated in the family program at the rehab and our relationship began anew.

At that time the pharmacy association did not have a formal program, and when I finished treatment my boss offered to reinstate me, but only with the approval of the rehab center. I consulted my therapist, who told me that he did not feel capable of making that decision, and called a meeting of two recovering doctors and one recovering nurse. I told them my story, and they said I would be crazy to put myself at risk of relapse by handling drugs so soon. On the basis of that, my therapist refused to authorize my returning to work in the drug store.

I was madder than hell at this. Here I had cooperated and was trying my best, but no one trusted me. However, I had no choice, so I took a job selling surgical supplies to hospitals. I went to NA meetings regularly and continued in outpatient therapy. After eighteen months of being clean, I went back to work in a drug store. All I can say is that I thank God I didn't go back any earlier. It was difficult enough handling drugs then, even after so long a period in recovery, so I'm sure that if I had tried earlier, I would have relapsed.

I've been clean for seven years. Kim and I have a great relationship. In the process of making amends, I told her about my other relationship. She was deeply hurt, and it took a good bit of time before we could work this out. I believe she trusts me now, not because she is naive but because I *can* be trusted. The only real difficulty I have is filling legitimate prescriptions for tranquilizers and pain pills when I know that these people are being addicted by their doctors, but there is nothing I can do about that.

I am actually grateful for my addiction, because it was the crisis that brought me and Kim to get honest with ourselves and decide what we wanted out of life and what we wanted with each other.

20

I Threw Three Strikes
and I'm Out

Sam McDowell, whose supersonic fast ball (responsible for his being referred to as "Sudden Sam") virtually assured him entry into the Baseball Hall of Fame, had his last drink in 1980. In order to help youngsters who might accept words of wisdom from a superstar, McDowell shed his anonymity and told the story of his successes and failures.

The details of McDowell's career are relatively unimportant and can be briefly encapsulated. Baseball scouts were highly impressed by his stunning fast ball, and upon graduation from high school at 17, he became an $85,000 bonus baby with the Cleveland Indians. Even though he subsequently led the American League in strikeouts five times and represented the League in six All Star games, he never pitched to his full potential, which he ascribes to his use of alcohol. It was said of him, "He has a million dollar arm and a ten-cent brain." Actually, Sam has an excellent brain, but its function was seriously compromised by alcohol.

McDowell played for a number of major league teams that were fascinated by his stellar pitching but were unable to put up with his alcoholic shenanigans. At the time of his release, he was still young enough to have paralyzed batters with his fast ball, but he was broken in body and spirit, penniless, with his dream of greatness shattered. He then left baseball to flounder for two more years in the throes of alcoholism before surrendering to recovery.

But let's hear Sam tell it.

Case 22: My Control (of My Fast Ball) Was Perfect

In my particular case and in the case of professional athletes, powerlessness and unmanageability are awesome topics to tackle. However, the need is long overdue and might prove beneficial in many areas, not just addiction alone. The way professional athletic teams operate may actually be conducive to the development and/or progression of addiction.

As you know, an athlete is totally trained and conditioned throughout his career. He is not powerless; he has all the power in the world to be whatever he wants, and that is his responsibility, since he is out there on the field by himself. Additionally, there are all the tricks of the trade, in which an individual can condition himself to believe that everything is manageable. For example, in my particular case and throughout my career, there were hundreds of instances where I could rationalize any of my behaviors and it would seem almost plausible, because as long as I was winning, there couldn't be anything wrong with Sam McDowell.

I was a functional, controlled drunk, so to speak. I went out after a game I'd pitched and drank into the wee hours of the morning and got drunk out of my mind. I did the same scenario the next night after the game and then assumed everything would be perfect if I did not drink for the next two days. I continued on this track for three-quarters of my baseball career.

Throughout my career, I had everybody and his brother constantly attempting to tell me that I had a drinking problem, that I should slow down, or that I just didn't know how to drink since I didn't drink like them. I could always come back and show them that I was the winning pitcher and they were losers and therefore, I must have the right idea. Under the heading "the games alcoholics play," one year I got so fed up with everyone including the general manager getting on my case, I decided to prove to them that I was not an alcoholic and quit drinking any alcoholic beverage whatsoever for the rest of the baseball season. I did not have a very successful time of it, either on the field or off.

The following year the team was convinced that I was not an alcoholic, since I could quit for that three-quarters of a year, and told me they knew I wasn't an alcoholic and therefore there was nothing wrong with my drinking. However, they had chosen to have the pitching coach go with me whenever and wherever I wanted to go out drinking in the hope that he could protect me against falling into a serious injury of some sort. Of course, the year they relented and let me go back to drinking was the best year I ever had in baseball, winning twenty games. Obviously, that was also my belief.

Among the hundreds of millions of promises and verbal contracts, I had made either to the baseball team, future baseball teams, or my wife and family that this wouldn't happen again, I continued to get intoxicated out of my mind, not realizing what I was doing, what I was not doing, or how I came about doing it since truly in my heart I had the greatest intentions of not drinking or embarrassing the family. In addition, I couldn't understand why this was causing me so many problems since I was a very strong-willed individual, to the point where I used to take bets with different teammates on willpower. Whether it was not eating desserts for six months or not smoking for two or three months, or not eating certain types of food, or running—whatever it was that had to deal with willpower, Sam McDowell always won. However, when it came down to controlling my drinking I was a failure. I went through every aspect of the geographical cure concept. I went through the changing of the drinks—so that I would switch from Scotch to Irish whiskey—thinking that was the problem—changing to beer only—thinking that was the problem—or vodka only. I truly believed in my heart that I'd found the final cure once and for all when I made those changes.

One of the things that was very powerful with me, was that I always rationalized the fact that I was a professional athlete and those individuals who were getting all over my case, whether it was my wife, my parents, my brothers, or personal friends, simply didn't know how to drink. They didn't understand that this was the life and image a professional baseball player is supposed to have. I was expected, as a celebrity, to be out in the public drinking all the time, and if they couldn't handle it like I could it was because they were wimps.

Although I put up a very strong pretense, I continually made promises to myself that this wasn't going to happen again, or that wasn't going to happen again, whether it was DWIs, or fights in bars and restaurants, or wrecking cars, or blackouts—sleeping in my car and waking up not knowing where I was or had been.

In my particular case, I firmly, with all of my heart, believed that it was some sort of a mental illness. At that time I didn't know anything about addiction, but continually saw other individuals who drank as much as I did and never got into trouble, or showed up late, or missed a ball game, or wrecked cars, or ruined their family life, or just lost everything. I could not understand how they could drink heavily and I couldn't without all of that happening to me. Therefore, I believed in my heart that I had some sort of a mental illness that embarrassed me to the point that I could never talk about it with anybody.

For most of my baseball career, I can conscientiously say I never spent much time on the fact that I may have been an alcoholic, except for the few instances where I was backed into a corner. Then of course, I would play my game of scheming and lying so that I could convince everybody, and myself as well, that I wasn't. This is when I tried to quit drinking for three months, six months, nine months, or a year, in order to prove to everybody that I was not an alcoholic. Of course, I would then get back to my usual drunken behavior.

During most of my baseball career, a good part of my time was taken up with excuses, rationalizations, and the entire game of why I did certain things to try and overcome the damage that I had done, to con myself out of jams, and so on. I can frankly say that very seldom would I ever try and take a look as to whether it might be alcoholism. It was obviously intentional, even if it was at the subconscious level, because I was able to continue making big money and because I continued to be "held in high esteem" as a celebrity. I never had to take a look at my behavior.

It was only near the end when the New York Yankees released me that I ever thought of trying to take a look that it might be alcoholism.

During the meeting dealing with my release, they explained to me that I was a drunk and that I would never get help for myself, never recover, and was finished in baseball. But, as it occurs with an alcoholic's scheming, I was able to immediately talk the Pittsburgh Pirates into permitting me to go to spring training and to give me a chance to make their team. Joe O'Brien, the general manager, acknowledged that he had heard rumors and understood that I was an alcoholic and told me I would be released with my very first drink. Even knowing that, I was able to rationalize that if I succeeded enough, if I could become a star on the team and if they needed me enough, I would be able to do anything I wanted to with my drinking. I am not saying that was a conscious thought at the time. However, looking back I do believe it was the ultimate subconscious plan.

Because I went to spring training with all of the greatest intentions in the world of not drinking and became so successful in spring training that I led the team in every category, I began sneaking out once in a while to have a couple of drinks. I truly believed that even if they found out that I was drinking, as long as I didn't get drunk I would be able to stay with the team. In fact, I knew that they knew I had been out drinking sometimes and yet they signed me to a contract anyhow and so I went north with the team. It was only after two major episodes, one in which I didn't show up at the ballpark for three days because I was so sick from one of my drunken episodes (here I convinced the team that I had the flu and even got a doctor to document this). The second was when I showed up drunk at the ballpark in New York after finishing one of the greatest relief appearances of my career (thinking that they couldn't do without me) that Joe O'Brien called me into his office and released me. He simply stated that I was an alcoholic out of control and they didn't know what to do with me.

McDowell then tried to make a living selling insurance, but his drinking interfered with this function as well. At the recommendation of a friend, McDowell consulted me, but only as a psychiatrist who would try to unravel the mystery of his emotional disorder. When I told Sam that his problem was alcohol, he politely left the office.

Like many others who refuse to acknowledge their addictive disease, I prayed for his enlightenment and recovery. A year after our first encounter, I came into Gateway Rehabilitation Center one day to find that Sam had admitted himself. I was grateful that my prayers had been answered, and that he sought treatment while his magnificent brain was still intact.

Sam has made an excellent recovery. It has by no means been easy, but once he made the turnaround, he put his colossal energies to constructive use, initially working with many youngsters who felt free to call him at home, day or night. Sam has since gone back to pitching baseball, but now he is not throwing a little missile at bewildered batters. Rather, he is pitching the message of recovery to athletes who, like himself, have become involved with chemicals that threaten their careers and very lives.

Every once in a while I tease Sam, telling him that it is time for him to shed a few pounds, get back into shape, and get back on the mound and throw his blazing fast ball. Sam smiles. He is no longer interested in striking out batters. Rather, he is doing his utmost to see that other athletes do not strike out in life.

21

Not Until the Bitter End

As was noted earlier, veterans in alcohol and drug rehabilitation say that a person does not recover until he has hit "rock bottom." This is a highly variable concept, there being "high bottoms" and "low bottoms." Most of the personal accounts included in this book are of the latter variety, with the individual not entering recovery until forced to do so by some overwhelming crisis. An example of a "high bottom" is Tom, who was a very prominent attorney. Tom's wife repeatedly asked him to curtail his drinking and when her words fell on deaf ears, she took her pillow out to the sofa saying, "I'm not going to break up the family, but it's all over between you and me." Whereas most alcoholics would have totally ignored this, this was "rock bottom" for Tom. When he told his office partner that he was going to get help for his drinking problem, the latter was taken by surprise. "What drinking problem? When do you drink?" Obviously, Tom's drinking had never manifested itself outside the home.

With many other addicts, the relationship with the chemical is reminiscent of marriage vows, to stick with the chemical "in sickness and health, for better or worse, until death do us part." There is usually more sickness than health, more often worse than better, and too often it is only death that tears the two asunder.

What happens along the way? Doctors, dentists, nurses, pharmacists, lawyers, educators—what about their patients and clients? What kind of services do they receive?

Strangely enough, they are usually well served. It is not until near the bitter end that work performance begins to show the impact of the chemical dependency. As one recovering physician said, "Who is the best doctor in North Carolina? Dr. Jones, when he is sober. Who is the second best doctor in North Carolina? Dr. Jones when he is drunk."

Case 23: Who Performed the Cesarean Sections?

On the fifteenth anniversary of his sobriety, Dr. B. shared his history with a group of recovering physicians.

"Back in those days, I was a member of an obstetric-gynecology group practice. One night I had been out drinking and when I arrived at the hospital the next morning, quite hung over, I was horrified to discover that there had been two cesarean sections and two deliveries on our service. It had been my night on call, and I had been out drinking all night.

"I had no idea how I was going to explain my absence to my partners. My head was throbbing with pain as I sat down to phone them, to make up some cockamamie excuse for my dereliction. Just as I was about to dial, my eyes lit upon a patient's chart. It was *my* handwriting. I looked at that chart and at the other three. I had done both cesareans and both deliveries myself! There were four healthy babies, four healthy mothers, and four perfectly documented charts. Everything had been performed admirably well, except for the fact that I had no recollection of it."

Dr. B. credited me with motivating him to recovery. He had been admitted for his fourth detoxification in the wee hours one morning, and when he was brought into the examining room for an interview, he was still quite toxic. I asked, "Paul, why don't you just sleep it off? I'll be back later and we can talk then."

Dr. B. said that he staggered back to his room, and was devastated by the thought, "I'm in such bad shape that Abe can't even talk with me," whereupon he fell to his knees and said, "God help me now."

At the risk of belaboring the point, the identity of many people is entirely contained in their profession or position. They may permit everything else to deteriorate but will protect their professional life until the very end.

Ron is a lawyer who knew he was subject to alcohol-induced memory lapses (blackouts), and he therefore recorded every conversation and kept a meticulous record of all details of transactions, knowing that he would forget them otherwise.

His case may be extreme, but it is quite common for alcoholics and drug addicts in the earlier stages of their addiction to deliver particularly high quality services. Precisely because they are aware of the possibility of impaired performance, and particularly because exposure might jeopardize their love affair with their chemical, they exercise extra caution that everything be done properly and that nothing be overlooked. They may be superefficient and these defensive maneuvers to conceal their addiction may result in the prolongation of their condition. It is not uncommon to hear an employer say, "He was the last person I would have suspected of being an alcoholic. His work was always of the highest caliber, and I wished I had more employees like him."

Early intervention may forestall the bitter end, or as we say, "raise the bottom." There are subtle signs that associates can detect and there are gross manifestations within the family that should lead to earlier diagnosis and treatment. The problem is that so often other individuals in the addict's environment are "codependent" or "enablers," and they allow the condition to progress to a bitter end. Let us now look at some of these codependent and enabling phenomena.

22

Enabling and Codependence

"Enabling" and "codependence" are sometimes used interchangeably. However, although there is some overlap, these two are really separate concepts.

"Enabling" refers to the behavior of people in the environment of the chemically dependent person that is conducive to continuation of the problem. It is important to distinguish "enabling" from "causing." As of yet, no one knows for certain the cause or causes of chemical dependency.

We may understand enabling with this analogy. Fire is *caused* by something igniting a flammable substance. The *cause* of the fire is the spark or the match. However, fire can burn only in the presence of oxygen; hence although oxygen does not *cause* a fire, it *enables* it to continue. Indeed, the reason we put out a fire with water is because dousing it prevents access of oxygen to the flame. With a small fire, this can also be accomplished by smothering it with a blanket.

This analogy is of particular importance in chemical dependency. The fire department does not respond to a call by looking for the match that ignited the flame. That approach would be worthless and result in total destruction of the house. The effective method is to douse the flame and deprive it of oxygen.

Similarly, looking for the cause of alcoholism or any other chemical dependency is of no more help in overcoming the problem than is looking for the match that started the fire. If those who are enabling will discontinue the enabling behavior, the likelihood is that the chemically dependent person will then seek help for his problem.

Enabling may consist of having the supper warm and serving it at 10 pm when the husband finally leaves the bar, instead of at 6 pm when he should be home from work. It may consist of silencing the children and stifling their healthy activity so as "not to provoke daddy." It may consist of chaperoning him at weddings and parties to try and control the amount of alcohol he consumes, or making excuses for him when he does not show up for work on time. It may consist of giving a son or daughter money for drugs so they won't steal or engage in prostitution. It may consist of paying off debts incurred on credit cards to obtain money for drugs, or paying for a lawyer to get the son or daughter out of jail. The possibilities of enabling are legion, but they essentially come down to a single point: the chemically dependent person is not permitted to suffer the consequences of his addiction.

In the final analysis, the factor most responsible for enabling of alcoholism or drug abuse is the lack of understanding of the condition and its natural course.

People whose will to live overrides every other consideration will allow themselves to be physically mutilated if doing so will preserve their lives. Countless people have undergone radical surgery for removal of a breast, lung, eye, arm, or leg because of the discovery of a relatively small malignant lesion. Parents of children, children of parents, spouses, and siblings in whose loved ones a cancerous growth was discovered, have submitted their loved ones to disfiguring surgery. If the patients resisted, relatives relentlessly pressured them to undergo a procedure that could save their lives, regardless of how radical it might be. They do so because they understand that untreated cancer is a killer, that it shows no respect for status or will or intelligence. They know that if neglected, the condition will progress and that every day of delay in instituting effective treatment reduces the likelihood of cure.

Case 24: They Might Think My Husband's Alcoholic

The wife of a physician who was chief of surgery in a suburban hospital consulted me because of her husband's drinking. He had denied he had an alcohol problem because he "only drinks beer." The beer consumption had progressively increased. "He comes home from the hospital, sits down in front of the television with a six-pack or more of beer, and that is where he wakes up the next morning. There is no communication between us, and he has not exchanged a single word with our son for months.

"So far he has managed to get to the hospital every day, although I don't know how he does it. But it is only a matter of time before he walks into the hospital drunk or is arrested for drunk driving and then he will lose his position and his practice."

I tried to explain to the woman the nature of progressive alcoholism and in order to help her get a better grasp of what to do, I scheduled a second appointment to be also attended by a recovering alcoholic surgeon.

When the doctor's wife began relating her problem to Dr. S. he listened politely and then stopped her. "You really don't have to go on, because you are describing me to a T. That was my course and I, too, refused to listen. I finally did come into the emergency room one night in a compromised state, and the administration insisted I see Dr. Twerski. I did so reluctantly but refused to accept his recommendations for treatment. Two years later I was kicked off the staff under the most embarrassing circumstances, and the condition I had wanted to hide was now announced by flashing neon signs. Just like you, my wife didn't know what to do. Had she gone to Al-Anon family group meetings, I might have come to my senses earlier and would have spared myself a great deal of grief. My suggestion is that my wife call you and you begin to go with her to Al-Anon meetings. From there on you will know what to do and what not to do, and I assure you that your husband will come around soon."

The doctor's wife said, "Oh, no. I could never go to Al-Anon meetings. What would happen if someone there recognized me and word got around that my husband has an alcohol problem. Why, he would lose all his patients, and we still have to put our son through college."

"But," I said, "you said yourself that it is only a matter of time before your husband exposes his problem by going to the hospital drunk. That exposure will be much worse than your being recognized at an Al-Anon meeting." My urging was to no avail. The doctor's wife was not amenable to logical argument and she refused to follow our recommendations.

"Codependency" is a broader concept that includes enabling, but has other features as well. Codependency has been variously defined but one of the better definitions is, "the chemically dependent person plays the tune and the codependents dance to it."

When the family adapts to the pathology of the drinker or user, behavior patterns no less sick than those of the chemically dependent person begin to emerge in sober family members. Various combinations of repressed and/or expressed anger, resentments, projection, and scapegoating result as both physical and emotional problems in the family members. Unrealistic responsibilities are thrust upon children, and growth potentials as well as social adaptation are stifled in an attempt to appease the addict or minimize the chemical use. Not infrequently, the family becomes sicker than the addict.

An example of the family illness of alcoholism or drug addiction follows:

Case 25: Carla

Alcohol was a part of my life for many years although I wasn't very aware of it. In talking with my parents I learned that drinking was definitely a contributor to the early deaths of both of my grandfathers. As I was growing up, my parents had parties and went to parties where almost everyone drank alcohol. At these times, I would notice my parents fighting more bitterly than usual, which I did not exactly connect with drinking. I remember my father getting sick sometimes, which I did connect with his drinking. It made me feel sad and worried about him.

I remember fights and yelling as I was growing up which I now realize stemmed from drinking. All it took was one member of the family to be drinking for the spouse and four children to all be in turmoil without even understanding what the turmoil was all about. I became used to feelings of anger, selfishness, self-pity, resentment, self-righteousness and, at the same time, inferiority. These feelings were normal to me. They were negative, but they were "comfortable." I was used to them.

I left home for college and things started out pretty well. I had many new clothes, a new hairstyle, and was feeling pretty good about myself on the basis of these outward things. I was attracting many dates, seemed to be popular, and was getting good grades. My self-esteem seemed to depend on whether or not I was attractive to the opposite sex.

If things were going good with some guy I was dating, part of me would get restless and create arguments. I would play hard to get for so long that the guy would finally get tired and move on, and then I would feel crushed and rejected. I decided to major in psychology, as I thought this would help me to figure out my ex-boyfriend and get him back and figure out myself!

As time went on, my grades fell to just passing, I was dating less, I was gaining weight, and my self-esteem was down. I was depressed most of the time. I thought if only I had my "dream man," everything in my life would be perfect. My goal in life was happiness and that depended on a man, or so I thought.

After graduation, things got better again for a while. My dating life got better, and I was feeling good about myself until the same pattern was repeated with some guy rejecting me, and then my world caved in again. I didn't know where to turn. At a friend's suggestion, I went to a psychiatrist and began many years of therapy for depression.

By the time I was 28, I thought I was an expert in human behavior. I had a master's degree in psychiatric social work. I had been to a number of therapists, worked as a social worker with families, and attended many workshops and seminars in the mental health field. At this time, I finally decided to get married. Since my husband was a psychiatrist, I really believed that between the two of us, any human problem could be solved!

You can imagine how confused and disturbed I was when we began to have problems and there seemed to be no solution. My husband drank a lot before our marriage, but I really paid this no mind. I thought this was how everybody lived. I drank a lot myself but he seemed to drink more than I did.

After we were married, the drinking bothered me more. At first, he would get all emotional about something, and I tried "social work" on him. This did a lot for my ego as though I, with my great insight, could be the therapist for a psychiatrist. As time went on, that ego trip wore down, though not completely. I got tired of reasoning with him about his drinking, because he wouldn't take my advice. I tried yelling, giving him the cold shoulder, throwing things, threatening to leave, begging for us to go to therapy to-gether—whatever I could think of. I knew drinking was a prob-lem, but I saw it as more a symptom of something wrong in the relationship or a deep-seated problem from the past.

I was slow to accept the idea of alcoholism. I thought alcohol-ism was something where you drank bottles each day, had DTs, and slurred your words all the time. I couldn't understand why anyone would wake up sick from drinking and take another drink. These things were not happening with my husband.

Once in a while though, like out of a fog, the thought would register that alcohol might be the reason for all our problems. I couldn't see what was happening to me. I spent my days sleeping late, watching soap operas, doing needlepoint, and waiting for our first child to arrive. I was rarely around other people.

When the baby came, I was an emotional wreck. I was filled with self-pity that my husband was so unavailable to me emotion-ally. He seemed so distant and cruel.

Shortly after the baby's birth, we moved to a new house. I was a real martyr. I did everything myself and was bitter, yet proud. I packed up just about everything and made sure I got the right movers.

By this time, I was willing to acknowledge alcohol as a definite problem in our life. I remembered reading the year before in a list of medical conventions about a meeting of International Doctors in Alcoholics Anonymous. This intrigued me at the time. Now I wondered if there was such a group where we lived. I called AA and asked them if there was a group of doctors in our area.

I thought, because of pride, my husband might not talk to just anybody in AA, but might be willing to talk to another profes-sional. I desperately wanted him to get help, and I finally was re-ferred to a psychiatrist in the AA doctors' group in our area. When I reached him by phone, he talked with me briefly and then asked his wife to talk to me. I thought he didn't understand the prob-lem, but I was the one who didn't understand.

His kind and generous wife helped me to attend Al-Anon meetings and spent much time just talking with me. She was so understanding. It was such a relief to talk to someone who knew exactly what I was going through. I didn't have to feel ashamed, embarrassed, or hypocritical. I could be myself and feel loved and accepted exactly the way I was.

This was the beginning of much growth and change for me. It was the beginning of learning to like myself and gaining self-respect as well as the respect of those around me. It was the beginning of learning to give love to others and to receive love. It was the beginning of freedom from despair.

I continued for about a year to try to control my husband's drinking. After I had tried everything I could think of, I gave up; I thought he was hopeless. I asked the God "of my understanding" to take over and "gave" my husband to Him. Within a week my husband sought help. He received treatment and began to attend AA meetings. We then both attended group therapy together.

I want to mention that my husband stopped drinking for nine months before he seriously got help. He was "dry," but there was no sobriety in our house. We were behaving just as if there was still active drinking going on. Removing the alcohol only leaves a great void that must be filled with some positive force in order to progress.

This was a difficult and threatening time for me. Although I hated the drinking days, sobriety was the real challenge. I had no excuse for not being a responsible, available wife. I did not trust my husband and did not want to be vulnerable to him. Though he was trying to reach out to me, I was very critical and judgmental of him for many months. Healing took time. But I can say with much gratitude and amazement that there is now peace and love in our home. There is sobriety and sanity.

As we received help from various sources, we began to heal physically, emotionally, and spiritually. We began to open our minds and hearts to each other and those in the world around us. By the grace of God, this healing process continues to set us free one day at a time.

Whether or not the alcoholic seeks or accepts help for his problem, family members can preserve their sanity by getting help for themselves. Qualified therapists familiar with alcoholism can provide vital counseling. Involvement in Al-Anon family groups can provide the support and benefit of the collective wisdom and experience that can enable family members to get off the vicious merry-go-round whose revolutions lead nowhere but to total dissolution.

23

A Lawyer's Codependents

As devastating as active alcoholism and drug addiction can be, once the family (the codependents as well as the user) recovers, a measure of serenity and the ability to be cheerful can be realized. The following letter of a woman to her friends demonstrates this.

Case 26: I Will Not Stick My Head in the Sand Again

Dear Roommates:

First of all, let me wish you a Merry Christmas and a Happy New Year! Only a few weeks late.

This has been an interesting time for me. I have all the usual Christmas-card good news. At the top of her class, Susie got into Cornell early decision. Sally is at the Academy as a fresh*woman*. She made the varsity field hockey team and is off to a good start academically. Jim has been appointed to the hospital board of trustees, in addition to his heavy case load at the law firm. I continue to be president of the Garden Society, teach Sunday school, and grow in leaps and bounds in my new position as director of public relations at Industries, Inc. I took the girls scuba diving (Jim doesn't scuba and refuses to learn) in the Caribbean last year and it was a fantastic vacation! We plan to return for Spring vacation. As you can tell, there are some good things happening in my little corner of the world.

When I went back to Penn for my 25th reunion last May, I was lucky enough to room with Jane (Hi Jane!). After I obsessively removed every one of the 50 or 60 old airline tags on her suitcase, she suggested that I was really compulsive and might need to see a therapist of some sort—that I had probably not gotten over many of the "issues" from my childhood. At that time I was feeling pretty darn good about my life and really couldn't understand why she was focusing on me. I wasn't the one saving luggage tags. (I *am* getting some help now, but more about that later.)

On the Saturday before Thanksgiving, my father called to tell me that he had a "little" liver problem. However, we were all going to meet for the holiday anyway at our old home in Philadelphia. So off we went. We arrived Tuesday, whereupon Sally announced to her grandfather that she really didn't like the Academy all that much and would like to transfer to Cornell (she had gotten in there as well) if it wasn't too much trouble.

On Wednesday Susie arrived at Dad's. Jim had spent the day in West Philadelphia, checking out his old haunts from his Penn days, as well as the local bars. He returned home half bombed. We all sat down to dinner. Susie (who is very withdrawn and often will offer no news of her life—I'm lucky if I get a phone call a month from her) could not stop telling us about her roommate who was in the process of being expelled for a drinking and driving episode at school. Jim's reaction was extreme. Shaking his wine glass at all of us, he yelled that if either child of his did such a thing, she would not go to college but straight into the Marines where she would learn what life was all about and appreciate how lucky she was. He then proceeded to get totally loaded. We survived Thanksgiving with all the nieces and nephews as well as Grandpa. By Saturday Dad was feeling so sick he went into the hospital. Then each member of my family left to go back to wherever until I was alone with my dad.

Finally, on Monday evening I took a taxi out to the airport where I went to the bookstore (where else?) and picked up a book called *How to Stop the One You Love from Drinking*, by Pinkam. (I knew that I could explain to anyone who asked that it was my father I was concerned about, because everyone knows what an alcoholic he is, but of course I was really thinking about Jim.) Well, the book flipped open to the discussion on the effect an alcoholic has on the rest of the family. I couldn't believe it! I always knew that too much alcohol was bad for the drinker, but I had no idea what a profound effect it had on the spouse and the children. Not only that, but often the children blame the nonalcoholic parent for not doing something about the alcoholic. Well, I was undone. Here I had been striving so hard to be the perfect mother and had failed miserably. Worst of all, I had not even recognized it. Luckily, the book explained that the reader should not feel guilty for whatever had occurred prior to her reading the book, but, if she did nothing after reading it, then the guilt should be intense. All I could think was: "What have I done to my kids?"

Jim met me at the airport but he was so loaded I had to drive home. I was so livid I decided I would not even unpack. Rather, I would leave the bags as they were because it would be easier to take them with me the next morning. Then I went into the guest bedroom (where I had been sleeping most nights for the last few months because of Jim's excessive drinking) to finish reading my new book, which warned against hasty decisions. The next morning I told him I wasn't leaving; however, I would be seeking counseling for myself, the girls and, hopefully, him. He said he would be willing, but would not go to a treatment center.

Later that morning a friend called me at work to ask how my dad was. I said not good, but I had another more pressing problem—and then I completely broke down. Well, she rushed right over and picked me up (keep in mind, I was relatively new at my job, but my boss could see I was going to be useless that day). After a day of catharsis (sobbing), I was able to get an appointment for the following Wednesday for Jim and me with the Number One guy in Pittsburgh on the subject of drugs and alcohol. I found this doctor through Jim's mom, because his older brother had been cross-addicted and had gone through rehab with this man.

That night I told Jim about my day, including the fact that I had told his mom about his addiction. Jim's anger was unreal, so I knew that I had found the one person who still really meant something to him. But he agreed to go to the appointment I had made. The next morning I had to repeat the whole conversation because Jim couldn't remember much of what I had said the night before. He still agreed to keep the appointment, however. And he stopped drinking.

Unfortunately, I had to fly out to see my dad in the hospital on the day of Jim's appointment, so I was unable to accompany him. But when I called the doctor the next day, he confirmed that Jim was indeed an alcoholic.

After seeing the doctor, Jim went back to drinking. I had wanted to solve all the problems over Christmas vacation (actually, I originally thought that one day of catharsis would be enough), but I now realize that just getting the subject of addiction out on the table and talking about it, especially with the girls (I took each one separately to a counselor who specializes in counseling for families of alcoholics), was achievement enough for that short period of time.

The girls returned to school after the holidays and then it was my turn. I'm seeing a counselor once a week. Right now I'm concentrating on slowing down, examining my feelings, and not "enabling." I go to Al-Anon twice a week as well. Jim refuses to stop drinking. To tell you the truth, we don't have anything left of our marriage at this point, but I have determined not to make any final decisions until this summer.

Naturally I have read dozens of books on various aspects of addiction: alcoholism, co-dependency, adult–child, parent–child, meetings, listening, love. While I feel Jim and I have been tremendously successful in raising two very intelligent, responsible young adults and developing our own intellectual natures, I have now come to realize where we have failed them and ourselves. Granted, neither one of us knew anything about addiction, nor did we come from homes that allowed us to recognize our feelings. But I have now come to see how essential this aspect of our lives is. As my counselor says, if you don't come to terms with your feelings, sooner or later you will become addicted (Jim) or nuts (me).

What else can I say? I have now told you the truth of what has been happening in my life over the last few months. I will not stick my head in the sand again. It is essential for all of us who want to get well to be able to see and say that the emperor has no clothes. I feel frightened and nervous about the future, but I also feel much calmer and more serene now that the truth is out and there are no more secrets. I hate secrets. Of course, I have also told my family. It's been very threatening and difficult for my parents to hear about addiction. But I refuse to be anything less than honest there, too.

I could go on and on about my latest crises and developments, plans for the future, and so forth but I think you get the picture. Thank you all for listening; it has really helped to get this out on paper.

Love,
Betsy

24

But Jews Don't Drink!
(A Rabbi's Story)

An internationally acclaimed expert on alcoholism stated in a lecture that the only ethnic group that is free of alcoholism is the Jews. I remarked to him that I know a number of people who must be masquerading as Jews. I know that they can't really be Jews because they're alcoholic!

It is unclear whether alcoholism among Jews is really a new phenomenon or rather that there is just a greater awareness of cases that had previously been covered up. Whatever the case, the fact is that the incidence of alcoholism among Jews is not negligible. At a retreat for recovering Jewish alcoholics, I heard a rabbi tell of his experience with alcohol.

"I am a staunch believer in tradition. The wisdom of the ages should not be dismissed lightly. Tradition has it that Jews are not alcoholic. Who was I to say that tradition was wrong?

"I had my first taste of alcohol when I was eight days old. There is a tradition to give the infant a few drops of wine to ease the pain of circumcision. Obviously it was believed that alcohol relieves pain. There is also a tradition that we celebrate special occasions with wine (you use alcohol when happy). As a firm adherent to tradition, I lived up to these two principles: alcohol to relieve pain and alcohol when happy. Since at any one time a person is either happy or sad, there was a strong tradition and good reason to use alcohol at all times, and I observed this religiously (oy).

"My home was not fanatically religious. My father was a salesman who worked out of his car and did not work on the Sabbath, and our home was kosher, but that was the extent of it. I went to public school and to after-school Hebrew classes to prepare for my bar mitzvah. I would go to the synagogue with my father on Friday nights, and I couldn't wait until the rabbi gave us a few sips of the sweet wine. I had a love affair with alcohol right from the beginning. When there were bar mitzvahs or other celebrations on Saturday morning, I used to help clear the tables. Everybody praised me for being such a good helper, but the real reason was that I could get to the wine or whiskey left over in the cups.

"As a child I dreamt of becoming a rabbi. I admired Rabbi Goldman with his distinguished silvery white hair and goatee. When Rabbi Goldman walked in everybody stood, and that's what I wanted: people to notice me, respect me, and stand up when I walked in.

"My parents pooh-poohed the idea. What kind of job was that for a good Jewish boy? Better I should be a doctor, a dentist, or at least a lawyer. I wasn't sure I wanted any of these. Doctors may make more money but nobody stands up when they walk in.

"If a psychoanalyst wants to dig for what happened to me in my childhood that caused me to become alcoholic, he'll come up empty handed. Nothing happened to me. My parents were good people and I had all the love and care a child could want. Geneticists might be luckier than psychoanalysts. There was my great-uncle Nathan, whose name was occasionally mentioned but quickly dismissed. In the planning for my bar mitzvah, I overheard my aunt asking whether Uncle Nathan would be invited, and my father butted in with a vehement 'No! I'm not going to have a *shikker* (drunkard) ruin our *simcha* (celebration).' So that's what it was! Uncle Nathan was a drunkard! Now being a drunk might be disgraceful enough, but you must understand that a *shikker* is not just a disgrace. It's a *shanda*. What is a *shanda?* If you take disgrace, shame, insult, and all their other synonyms and multiply them by twenty-five, you might approach the opprobrium of a *shanda*. And that's what it was to be a *shikker*. No other behavior is as loathsome or as abominable. When you say, "He is a *shikker*," you say it with the tone that indicates the person is about eight levels below Bluebeard. While it is certainly wrong to steal and a *goniff* (thief) is a bad person, the tone of voice in saying someone is a *goniff* does not approach that of saying he is a *shikker*. The abominable Uncle Nathan would not be allowed to defile my bar mitzvah. The thought that I could ever become a despicable *shikker* was beyond absurdity.

"I occasionally got drunk at high school parties and more often at college fraternities, but it was no big deal. For some reason I went to business school to become an accountant, but after the first year I quit and told my parents that their son was going to become a rabbi after all, and I was accepted in seminary. At this point, my drinking was still under fair control. Occasional drunks, but that's all.

"When I graduated seminary I found that the job market for rabbis was not the greatest, but the army needed chaplains. The pay was good and I could start off with a commission. Even if I didn't yet warrant people standing up for me, at least the enlisted men would salute me.

"Army life was tolerable. As a commissioned officer, I had access to the officers' club, where alcohol was in abundance, and no one took any notice of you unless you were *not* drinking. I drank more often and more heavily, and even had a few blackouts, but these were of no consequence.

"After four years in the army I began to get a bit tired of it, and sent out resumés to synagogues. With the additional credentials of an army officer, I began to get some responses. I auditioned at two synagogues and was favorably received, but then I was ordered to go to Vietnam. I could have gotten out of it, but felt it was not the right thing to do.

"Vietnam was ugly. Whatever you hear about its ugliness is only an understatement. The morale was terrible and many of the guys were on heroin. I was supposed to be a source of moral support and spirituality, but I was more doused in spirits than imbued with spirituality. I drank, I had blackouts, but no one paid any attention. Once I was sent out with a couple of guys on a mission and I was supposed to read the map and direct them. I had been drinking and got everything messed up, so that a mission that was to take two hours ended up taking nine. When we returned it was discovered that we had actually wandered behind enemy lines, so I received a medal for bravery.

"I kept in contact with one of the synagogues and they sent me a contract. I showed the contract to my commanding officer and told him how desperately I was needed back home. He was able to arrange my discharge from the army. The day I was supposed to leave Vietnam, I received a notice to report to headquarters, and was told I could not leave until I returned the bus I had signed out.

"Bus? What bus? I had no recollection of ever taking out a bus! But there was my signature and I had in fact signed out a bus. When and for what, I didn't have the slightest idea. It took a call to my congressman to get the army off my back.

"I came back to the States to accept my position as a rabbi. My drinking slowed up considerably, and I behaved exceptionally well. I loved the congregation, and in turn they took an interest in their young unmarried rabbi. Within six months I was married to a lovely young woman, and one year later our twin girls were born.

"Somehow around this time my drinking picked up again. Stress is no excuse, but it's as good as any when you need one. We were building a new temple, and I was under pressure to oversee the planning and construction, but most importantly, to raise the funds. I had to organize and schedule fund-raising events and solicit money, which I abhorred. *Schnorring* (soliciting) was easier to do when I felt relaxed and alcohol was a great relaxant.

"My drinking got worse; I had blackouts, and my dear wife was beside herself. She covered up for me and I got away with it. But I was getting depressed, slacking off work, and becoming impossible to live with. At my wife's insistence I saw a psychiatrist who diagnosed depression and gave me pills that I gladly took, but I continued to drink. My depression got worse and my wife insisted I get a second opinion. The second psychiatrist listened to me, took me to the window, looked at my eyes and said, 'Oh my God, you're jaundiced. Do you drink?'

"I don't know why but I admitted my drinking to him. Perhaps it was the grace of God. The doctor told me that no pills would help me if I drank, and if I stopped drinking I might not be depressed. He suggested that I take a medical leave and go to a rehabilitation center for a month. Later I discovered that he had suggested this in collusion with my wife, for which I will always be grateful. I had a good laugh at the rehab when they showed a film by an internationally known authority on alcoholism, who stated that the only ethnic group free of alcoholism were the Jews. I had to come to terms with the fact that I was the same abomination as Uncle Nathan: a *shikker*. I cried my eyes out about the depth to which I had sunk, but my therapist helped me realize that both Uncle Nathan and I were sick people, who could be helped to recover if we wished to.

"When I returned from the rehab, the first thing I did was call a meeting of the board of directors of the congregation, told them I was an alcoholic in recovery, and offered to resign. I was prepared to see the shocked expression on their faces, but instead they said, 'We knew of your alcohol problem all along, rabbi, but we just didn't know how to put it to you.' The next Saturday I gave a sermon on alcoholism, and for the first time in its history the congregation responded with a standing ovation. Even Rabbi Goldman never merited that!

"I've been sober for five years. I have weekly AA meetings in my congregation, and the children who attend Friday night services get grape juice instead of wine.

"I am grateful to God not only for the opportunity to recover, but even for the fact that I am an alcoholic. I don't know how many rabbis have the kind of relationship with their congregants that I do. As someone who knows what raw feelings are like, I can be mindful of how other people may be hurting. I am their rabbi, they are my flock, and we need each other."

25

Controlled Social Drinking?
(A Priest's Story)

Can a recovering alcoholic go back to social drinking again? The overwhelming opinion of people who have worked with alcoholics or other chemical-dependent individuals is that there is no return to safe drinking again.

Years ago there was a study that claimed that a certain percentage of alcoholics could go back to safe, controlled drinking again. The percentage is irrelevant. Every alcoholic who wanted to drink again promptly seized upon this information to justify his use of alcohol. Several years later there was a follow-up by the same research group that stated their conclusions had been premature, and that those alcoholics who had been assumed to be using alcohol responsibly had again deteriorated into uncontrolled drinking.

So what does it mean if a person with an alcohol problem has been dry for a year or two? It means only that he has been dry for a year or two, and this should not be interpreted to mean that the alcohol problem has been cured. People who have had a problem with alcohol should abstain from alcohol indefinitely. Furthermore, since cross addiction is a fact of life, they should also avoid use of any other recreational drug. In the event that they must receive an addictive-type drug as part of medical treatment, they must take great precautions to avoid falling back into a full-blown relapse.

Nothing illustrates the fallacy of a return to safe drinking as well as the following account by a priest who is in recovery.

"Both of my parents were born in Ireland. My father was for all practical purposes a teetotaler and my mother was abstemious. Our Roman Catholic faith was very important and it was the very center of our family life. I owe my vocation to the priesthood to several individuals, but if I made a list of them my parents would be at the top.

"I had no problem with alcohol during high school, college, or the seminary. When I first came to the Fellowship of Alcoholics Anonymous I used to say that I could not recall any problems with drinking until my mid-fifties but I now realize that my drinking was not normal even during the first year after my ordination.

"I was ordained in 1950 and was assigned as an assistant to the pastor (there were three of us) in a middle-class parish in the northern section of Queens, New York. Almost every parishioner was a home owner. No one was wealthy but we had very few indigent people in the parish. It was a great place and the people were warm, friendly, and involved in parish life.

"After about five years there my problem drinking was becoming noticeable to my family and to some of the parishioners. A few reported their concerns to the pastor who spoke to me about it. I denied that there was a problem and I thanked him for his concern. Actually I was very angry at the parishioners and at him.

"During this five-year-period my priest friends had also become concerned about my drinking. I was the one who could not find my car or who had to be driven home after clerical gatherings. When the pastor first spoke to me I determined that I would never drink again. I kept that promise for about two years, acquiring the reputation of someone who had solved his problem.

"After this dry period I began to drink again—only a glass of wine at a meal now and then. No problem—so the drinking increased until the pastor and I had another little talk. Again I stopped but this time the dry period lasted only about a year and a half. The next time it lasted a year, then six months. The non-drinking periods were getting shorter and shorter and I had also become a closet drinker.

"At the time of my tenth anniversary of ordination, the pastor asked the bishop to transfer me to another parish. I left and took up my new assignment determined that I would never drink again. My determination lasted two years. The next period of non-drinking lasted about eighteen months, then a year, and then six months. Although these dry periods were similar to the ones already described, I was not able to see any kind of pattern developing but it is very clear to me now.

"At the end of an eight-year-assignment in this second parish the secretary for personnel called me and said the bishop wanted me to cover a situation in Queens where the pastor was drinking. I received this call during one of my dry periods, and because my drinking was now secret and periodic, everyone at the diocesan level thought I had solved my problem—so what better person than a recovered drunk to send to the drinking pastor in Queens?

"I arrived at this parish and within two months I'd gotten the pastor into treatment for his alcoholism. After a month at this treatment center, he returned to the parish on a Tuesday and by Wednesday he was a fall-down drunk. When he sobered up he told me that he wanted to resign as pastor and return to be chaplain in the hospital where he had worked before. He did so and I was appointed pastor.

"I didn't touch a drink for two years. Then I began having some wine at meals. Well . . . you know the pattern that developed: the dry periods got shorter and shorter. I was able to keep it from most of the parishioners because I was now the pastor and could go off for a few days to detox and leave my associate in charge. He had to be let in on my terrible secret, of course, and he was a very unhappy young man but went along with this for a while.

"One Saturday night when I went searching for him to say the 7 pm Mass in my place because I was in no shape to appear in church, I could not find him! He knew I was drinking and he suspected that I might ask so he just got lost. It was the best thing he could have done for me! Not to put too fine a point on it, the Mass was a disaster.

"After Mass I packed a bag and ran off to one of the hotels near Kennedy Airport. When I got to the hotel I called my secretary and let her know where I was. I was left alone all day Sunday while I 'tapered off' on beer at the hotel bar. On Monday morning my associate called and made two demands of me. He insisted that I get medical help, that I enter AA. I agreed but I didn't plan to be at the hotel when he arrived to take me wherever he wanted to take me.

"He was wise enough to know that I probably would run out on him, so he had another priest on the road a few minutes away from the hotel when he made his call to me. I was trapped! I was taken to a program in Manhattan and to Cabrini Hospital Detox Unit.

"It seemed to take forever to be admitted to the hospital. I was in very bad physical shape because I was at the beginning of the withdrawal process. I suggested to the priest who had driven me to the hospital that he could leave now because I could certainly take care of myself. Thank God he did not leave because he must have known that given half a chance I would dash out to the nearest bar. I finally got up to my room and was feeling as low as I have ever felt in my life when one of the orderlies asked me if I was ready to attend my first AA meeting. I thought I was in no shape to attend anything but my wake! However, I thought and I believe this was a great Grace from God that if this was what I would have to do to get sober then this was what I would do!

"As the years passed in the Fellowship of AA I gradually began to realize that my problem was that I could not handle success. I never seemed to turn to the bottle when I was faced with a problem; I turned to the bottle only to reward myself after I had coped with the problem. This was certainly true in my second and third (final) assignments. It took about two years in my second assignment to feel comfortable with the new parishioners and with the programs I was attempting to run for them. As soon as I felt at home and saw some good results in my work, I rewarded myself with a glass of wine at dinner.

"In my third assignment I discovered that it took me about two years to feel comfortable in the place and with the work, and again I rewarded myself with a little wine at dinner. I also realize today that the amount of wine I took when saying Mass was much more than I should have taken. It became my morning drink and as time went on it became the spark to the fuse of my alcoholism.

"I will always be grateful to my associate for having the courage to stand up to me and make those two demands of me. I have never, for one moment, been tempted to drink since I entered that detox ward in lower Manhattan. I have only one very minor regret: When I drank, I wanted to drink as a gentleman but because I am a victim of an insidious and fatal disease I only drank as a drunk. It is, as I've said, a very minor regret."

26

Beginning Recovery

If the chemically dependent person recognizes the problem and is willing to consider a recovery program, the first step is to contact a competent alcoholism and drug counselor for an evaluation and recommendation of an appropriate treatment program. In contrast to the treatment plans of the past, programs can now be tailored to the individual's needs. They do not necessarily require residential treatment, and may even allow the individual to continue in his occupation.

It is highly advisable to contact one's own advocacy group, and in the Appendix I've listed some contacts for doctors, lawyers, pharmacists, dentists, and nurses groups. If you don't know how to reach one of these groups in your state, the alcoholism and drug counselor can usually get the desired information.

It is also advisable to register formally with the advocacy group, since various problems may arise that can be addressed more effectively by those who have had greater experience. There may also be some legal advantages. For example, the biannual license renewal application for Pennsylvania physicians asks whether you have ever had or been treated for a substance abuse problem. If you conceal this fact, you are at risk of having it discovered at some later date, and there is virtually no defense for willfully falsifying information on an application. Many people feel, with some justification, that if they answer in the affirmative, they are opening a Pandora's box. There is therefore a provision in the Pennsylvania application that if one is registered with the Physician's Health Program, one may answer "no," and it will not be considered fraudulent.

Where such stipulations are lacking, many people are tempted to answer the question in the negative. This is unwise for the reason stated above. Should the truth emerge at some later date, you may find your license and malpractice insurance in jeopardy.

If the chemically dependent person refuses to seek treatment, family members, particularly the spouse, should avail themselves of counseling with an alcoholism and drug family counselor, and it would also be wise to attend Al-Anon or Nar-Anon family support groups.

The counselor's evaluation may sometimes result in recommendation of an intervention. This essentially consists of confronting the chemically dependent person with the problem and also clarifying the positions of the significant others.

Intervention requires careful planning. Participants should include concerned family members, the alcoholism and drug counselor, and may also include some significant others, such as employer, partner, pastor, or friends who wish to help. Whereas the chemically dependent person may deny each person's allegation individually, it is much more difficult to deny the evidence presented by a number of people simultaneously.

The intervention should be rehearsed with the alcoholism and drug counselor, so that each person is properly prepared to respond to expected denials. The family and significant others should be prepared to state what their position is if the chemically dependent person refuses to accept help with the problem. For example, is the wife willing to continue the relationship if the husband refuses help? Empty threats are most unwise, and if the wife is sincerely determined to leave if the addiction continues, she may say so, but if she is in doubt as to whether she would do this, she should not make an empty threat. Is the partner or employer willing to continue the relationship without the person seeking treatment? What happens if the person says, "All right. I will never touch another drop. I swear it. But I'm not going to any treatment program." What does one do then? All bases must be covered, because if there is any weak spot in the wall, the chemically dependent person is certain to find it and break through.

Will such an intervention arouse much anger and hostility especially toward the family? Yes, it will do so initially, but almost without exception the anger abates, and the individual is eventually grateful that people were sufficiently interested in his welfare and survival to prevent his continuing on a self-destructive course.

Case 27: I Deserve to Have My Daddy at My Graduation

The wife of a 56-year-old physician consulted me because of his heavy drinking. He was in total denial that he had a problem, although there had been frequent alcohol-induced arguments. He had been stopped for drunk driving twice, but each time friendly police officers who knew him personally drove him home and said, "Be careful, Doc, one day you won't be able to get away with it." She had contacted the state medical society physician's program, and one doctor had called to talk with him, but he politely (or not too politely) refused the offer, then tore into his wife for trying to ruin him by turning him over to the authorities.

They had two sons, who were both away at college, and one daughter at home. The only way to convene the entire family was when the boys came home for Thanksgiving, some five weeks away. During this time we had several conference calls in which the sons participated in rehearsing the intervention.

The day before Thanksgiving I told the wife to notify me when her husband was not intoxicated, since there is no point in trying to talk sense to an inebriated person. When I got the call, I went to their home accompanied by a recovering physician whom I had informed about the case.

The doctor and his family were all in the living room when we walked in and although clearly irritated, he managed to remain calm. I told him that we had no ties to any official body and that we were there solely to help him. He denied he needed help, and that everyone was making a mountain out of a molehill.

One son spoke up, "Dad there are times when I can't understand a single word you say on the phone because your speech is so slurred." The other son said, "I've told you things you've said to me that you have no memory of saying. When I told you I received a delinquency notice on my tuition and that I would not be permitted to take an exam, you promised to send the check out the next day. I was refused entrance to the exam and you claimed I had never mentioned it to you. You're having blackouts, Dad."

His wife then mentioned several unpleasant incidents resulting from his drinking, although she was careful not to mention those that would have humiliated him. The recovering doctor said, "Look, Pat, I know what you're going through. I wish my family had taken this step before I went over an embankment in my car and the accident was splattered all over the papers. That was the last of my anonymity, let alone the injuries that took me out of commission for six months."

Dr. Pat got up and quite angrily said, "Okay, if that's the way you feel about it, I won't touch another drop for the rest of my life. But you're not going to get me to go to any meetings with a bunch of drunks. I'm not going to declare myself an alcoholic, which I'm not, and lose all my patients just to satisfy you people."

The recovering doctor countered, "Pat I haven't lost even a single patient. After I came back into practice all my patients returned, even though some of them had to go to another doctor when I was laid up, and by then everyone knew I was alcoholic. I go to AA meetings right in my neighborhood, and I do meet some of my patients there."

Dr. Pat paced up and down the room. "That may have been okay for you, but it's not for me. Forget it."

At this point, Amy, 15, began crying. "I'm going to graduate from high school in two years and all the other kids will have their fathers there. I deserve to have my father there, too. You're not being fair to us, Daddy."

At this point Dr. Pat sat down and began crying. The family assembled around him with abundant hugging and kissing. After the emotions subsided, Dr. Pat looked up at me, "Okay, Abe. You win. Where and when do I go?"

"No, Pat," I said. "You're the winner. And there are several treatment facilities you can choose from."

This episode occurred eleven years ago. Dr. Pat has been sober since, his practice is thriving, and he couldn't care less about whether anyone knows he is an alcoholic.

Most interventions do lead to treatment, but sometimes the chemically dependent person is adamant in his refusal. At such times the family and others might have to implement what they've threatened to do. The wife may leave or the partners may ask that he leave the group practice. Incidentally, in preparation for such an intervention, all parties should seek legal counsel about the actions they may have to take.

And then what? Isn't it possible that with his world falling apart, the chemically dependent person may commit suicide? While suicide is a rare occurrence, it cannot be ruled out. An unsuccessful intervention and its aftermath may lead to desperate actions. But the family must consider the options. Whereas suicide is a dreaded possibility, the likelihood is small. The results of wholesale disaster from unchecked addiction are much, much greater.

If the chemically dependent person accepts treatment, the family will undoubtedly heave a sigh of relief. But while a positive first step has been taken, it is premature to celebrate. Recovery is an extended process and will test everyone's patience and stamina. Certainly the attitude, "Well, now that he's in treatment, we can all relax," is not justified. As has been indicated, addiction involves and affects the entire family, and all family members should be ready to participate in whatever the treatment facility recommends. With patience and perseverance treatment can result not only in sobriety, but in a better, more efficient, and happier function of the entire family.

27

Making the Change

It is difficult to describe all that transpires in treatment, whether it takes place in a residential setting or in one of the varieties of outpatient treatment. However, here we focus on some principles of recovery.

One recovering alcoholic, on the twenty-fifth anniversary of his sobriety, began his talk by saying, "The man I *was* drank, and the man I *was* will drink again." In other words, sobriety requires a transformation of character. Abstinence alone, without significant changes in one's personality makeup, is almost certain to result in relapse.

The term *rehabilitation* was borrowed from physical medicine, where it is appropriate. If a person was functioning well until he suffered a stroke or was injured in an accident that resulted in loss of function of a limb, the goal of rehabilitation is to restore the limb to its pre-morbid state. Restoration of 80 percent function is considered a major achievement, and restoring 100 percent function is outstanding.

This is not true of addiction. Take the case of a person who developed alcoholism at age 30. Prior to that he drank occasionally and moderately and had no untoward effects from alcohol. Something about this person, the totality of his physiologic and psychologic aspects, resulted in his developing a progressive alcoholism problem.

Let's assume that he enters treatment at age 39. If treatment succeeds in restoring him to the pre-morbid stage or the pre-alcoholic person he was at age 30, *nothing* has been accomplished, because it was *that* person who went on to become alcoholic. Complete restoration to the pre-morbid stage, which would be considered a 100 percent *success* in physical rehabilitation, is a 100 percent *failure* in addiction rehabilitation.

It is clear, then, that what must emerge from the recovery process is not only an abstinent person, but a person whose character and personality are substantially different from the pre-addiction phase. This change cannot occur over a brief period even with the most intensive treatment, but is rather a gradual change that may take years, and it is this change that comprises true sobriety. Abstinence without characterologic change is referred to as "dry drunk."

Tom was a very fine attorney who abstained from alcohol to avoid the breakup of his marriage, but refused to attend AA. After Tom was abstinent for three years, an attorney friend with many years of sobriety prevailed upon him to give AA a try. Tom eventually became very involved in the program and we became close friends. On his seventeenth anniversary I called to congratulate him. "How does it feel to be seventeen years sober?" I asked. "That's not quite accurate, doctor," Tom replied. "I'm seventeen years *dry*, but only fourteen years *sober*. Those first three years I hung onto abstinence by my fingernails, and they were miserable years. Had I not gotten into AA, I'm sure Ellen would have left me after the kids grew up because I was impossible to live with."

From what we have said earlier in regard to the role of a negative self-image in addiction, it follows that one of the psychological components that must undergo change is the self-concept. In addition to the feelings of inadequacy and unworthiness that antedated the onset of the addiction, many of the sequelae of addiction further depress the self-image. Proper psychotherapy for the addiction, in addition to a Twelve Step program, can bring about the necessary changes. The Fourth Step in the program, which consists of a thorough moral inventory, and the Fifth Step, which requires frankly sharing everything about oneself with another person, are the beginnings of self-awareness. Changes in conduct such as becoming rigorously honest, making amends, and helping others in recovery can significantly elevate a person's self-esteem.

As sobriety continues various self-destructive habits are eliminated and character traits improve. The recovering person begins to function better and cope much more efficiently with various challenges in life. This results in further enhancement of one's self-image and self-confidence.

These changes do not occur overnight. Years of negative self-feelings and addictive thinking and behavior cannot be reversed rapidly, but changes do occur over a period of time. Addictive thinking can persist even in abstinence, and is replaced by healthy thinking only very gradually. In my book *Addictive Thinking* (1990) there is a description of the unique type of thinking characteristic of the addict.

The emergence of a new personality is not without risks. As we have noted, it does not suffice to go back to the pre-addictive personality, for the person who emerges in recovery is truly another person, and while this new person is a much healthier one, it may present a problem.

Let us suppose that when John and Mary met they were 23 and 21 respectively. They fell in love because they were very compatible, which means that each one accommodated to and complemented the other's needs. John had been a rather quiet, passive person since childhood. He was a follower rather than a leader and did not like to make waves. He lacked self-confidence and was more comfortable with others making decisions for him. He was employed as a bookkeeper, and led an uneventful life.

Mary was a much more assertive person. She is an interior decorator and likes to dictate to people what should please them and how they should spend their money. John and Mary hit it off from the beginning. Mary liked to lead and John liked to follow. Mary liked to make decisions for everyone else, and John liked everyone else to make decisions for him. Who could ask for a better match?

At age 30, John was introduced to cocaine and before long he was a fairly regular user. Together with cocaine came increased use of alcohol. The addiction ran its course and at age 36, John was admitted to a treatment program. His program emphasized self-awareness and correcting faulty habits. It became evident that John's passivity and docile temperament were the results of a negative self-image that began in childhood. In time his self-esteem began to improve and as a result he began to be much more assertive. He was no longer happy with assigning all the decision making to Mary and insisted that some things be done his way.

But, this is not quite what she had bargained for. Had she wanted a more assertive husband, she would not have married John. Because John is now psychologically a healthier person this is no longer a comfortable relationship. As John continues to improve the couple's compatibility begins to deteriorate.

If Mary becomes involved in some type of family counseling, particularly with the Al-Anon family program, she may also make some changes in her self, concomitant with John's. For example, she may discover why *she* has the need to make decisions for everyone. Perhaps this is her way of dealing with her own feelings of inferiority. As I point out in my book *Life's Too Short* (1995), some people with a negative self-image may try to overcome these distressing feelings by becoming domineering. If this is true of Mary, then she may able to drop this defensive mechanism as her self-esteem improves. John and Mary can become compatible again, but this time on a different level.

Sobriety and recovery are growth processes. If both partners participate in growth, they may have an excellent relationship. If only one of the two grows, a disparity may develop which can threaten continuity of the relationship.

Another major component of recovery is *spirituality*. Spiritual development may or may not proceed along religious lines. In my book *I'd Like to Call for Help, But I Don't Know the Number* (1996), I explained that people who have no religious affiliation whatever can nevertheless be very spiritual people.

The *spirit* may be thought of as comprised of those features that are unique to human beings and that distinguish man from animals. Among these are the abilities (1) to learn from history, (2) to reflect on the purpose of one's existence, (3) to think about self-improvement, (4) to make salutary changes in oneself, (5) to consider the consequences of one's actions, (6) to delay gratification, and (7) to make moral, free decisions.

It is readily apparent that animals do not have these capacities. Taken together, all these abilities that are unique to man may be thought of as constituting the human *spirit*. A person who believes in Creation may believe that this spirit was instilled in man by God, while as someone who is an atheist may believe that all these capacities developed in man as part of the evolutionary process.

When a person exercises these unique human capacities, he is being *spiritual*. Thus, spirituality is nothing other than making the most of one's human uniqueness. Further elaboration of this important theme can be found in the work cited, where it is demonstrated that all these components of the spirit are neglected during active addiction and must be reclaimed and implemented if stable sobriety is to occur.

It should be evident that the salutary changes that occur in a person who takes his recovery seriously result not only in elimination of various problems incident to chemical dependency, but also in significant improvements in his relationships and overall functioning.

28

Coming Back

When the addiction has been exposed and the chemically dependent person returns to his previous societal position, there may be
some difficulties in reentry. Some difficulties may be fantasied, but
others may be real.

The exact incidence of chemical dependency among professionals is unknown, but it is estimated that among physicians, for example, one out of fifteen is chemically dependent. In certain spe-
cialties, such as anesthesiology, the incidence is thought to be
higher. The chemically dependent person whose problem has *not*
been exposed may actually present a greater risk than the one who
has been identified. But of course, when you don't know that a
person has a problem, you can't do anything about it. Once the
problem has been identified, it is obvious that certain precautions
must be taken to protect the health and welfare of patients and
clients.

Professional associations have agreements with the recovering
chemically dependent person whereby necessary safeguards are
provided, such as periodic urine testing and other monitoring pro-

cedures. These may continue for several years until the high risk period has passed.

In returning to one's position, one may encounter the "fishbowl syndrome," which derives its name from the common practice of watching the movements of the fish in a fishbowl. Similarly, the recovering professional may feel that his every move is being watched. This may indeed be true and is certainly a very distressing feeling. Fortunately, after several weeks, the fishbowl syndrome begins to wane.

In spite of society's more enlightened attitude toward addiction, the recovering professional may still encounter some negativity that makes reentry uncomfortable. He may be viewed with suspicion and mistrust. Participation in the professional support groups may be very effective in helping the recovering person deal with such obstacles.

One very competent surgeon applied for staff privileges at a hospital but was rejected because of his history of addiction. He appealed the decision and asked me to attend the hearing as a support person. I suggested to the committee that inasmuch as there had recently been some adverse publicity on physician impairment due to drugs and alcohol, they could assure the public that all physicians doing surgery in their particular facility were free of any chemical problem. This could be accomplished by asking every physician entering the surgical suite to submit a urine specimen for a drug screen. "I can assure you that virtually all the surgeons on your staff would refuse to comply. The only one who will gladly comply is this applicant."

Recovering people feel that they are considered guilty until proven innocent. Given the high rate of relapse among addicts, one cannot be totally critical of this attitude. It is important, therefore, that the recovering person behave in a manner that will place him above suspicion.

While urine tests are generally reliable, the possibility of an error in the chain of custody of the specimen or even someone tampering with the sample must be considered. A positive urine sample in a recovering professional person can have grave consequences and inaccurate reports must be prevented. I know of one case where a physician had made some enemies during his active addiction, and when he submitted a urine specimen to the hospital laboratory, one of his enemies put a few drops of morphine in the sample, expecting that a positive test would result in his being dismissed from the staff. Fortunately, the tampering was easily detected, since opiate use never shows up in the urine as morphine, but rather as one of the metabolites. Although such tampering is certainly rare, the fact that a false positive can ruin a person's career justifies taking protective action.

My recommendation to recovering professionals is to have an independent test performed at a reliable laboratory *on the same day* that a specimen is submitted for monitoring. In the event of a false positive, one can present evidence that he was indeed free of drugs, and that the positive report was an error.

In many states there are advocacy groups for licensed professionals. These groups are very helpful in providing information about treatment resources, and they can also arrange for monitoring, which is often required for preservation of one's license. The advocacy group can write a contract with the client, spelling out the conditions for a recovery program, and state licensure boards generally honor these contracts.

The advocacy group may also be helpful in preserving confidentiality. For example, the Pennsylvania medical license renewal form has the question, "Were you ever treated for alcoholism or drug addiction?" Recovering physicians are in a dilemma, because to answer "no" is not only fraudulent but is also fraught with great risk, because if it is detected, they may lose their licenses, and in the event of a malpractice suit, they may find themselves not covered by insurance. On the other hand, doctors may feel that to answer "yes" may open a Pandora's box of investigations. However, on the renewal form there is a parenthetical remark, "(If you are registered with the Physician's Health Program [e.g. the Impaired Physicians' Program] you may answer 'no')." This provides an easy way out of the dilemma. As long as one is under supervision, "no" will not be taken as an untruthful answer.

It is understandable that the recovering person may have much anxiety upon returning to work. One surgeon stated, "The walk down the hospital corridor toward the operating room on my first day back was the longest walk I ever took in my life." Advocacy groups or therapists can help ease this anxiety by arranging for support from peers in recovery.

One of the purposes for including personal accounts in this book is because they all describe individuals who returned to their normal function after entering recovery. This should be reassuring to the person who fears that acknowledging the disease and accepting treatment will jeopardize his career. The only real danger to one's career is allowing the addiction to remain untreated.

29

What About
an Intervention?

An intervention is a technique essentially used to coerce a chemically dependent person into treatment when he refuses to do so on his own. It consists of a confrontation by a number of people whose relationship he values and by one or more helpers.

There is a monograph on intervention available from the Johnson Institute (Johnson 1996) that discusses the process in detail. Here we will note a few of the highlights.

As a rule, the more people who can participate in the intervention the better. These must be people who genuinely care for the individual and wish to extricate him from the self-defeating and self-destructive addiction. These are usually family members—spouse, children, parents, siblings—one or more very close friends who know of the problem and, if possible, the person's employer or business partner, spiritual advisor, and perhaps his physician. Each person must have personal knowledge of the addiction and have observed its effects on him or have reliable evidence of its detrimental consequences.

When confronted with any facet of his addictive behavior, the chemically dependent person may shrewdly rationalize and try to point out that alcohol/drugs were not the cause of the particular negative consequence. At the intervention, each person may present his observation of the addictive behavior, and when such evidence is presented from so many different directions, it is difficult for the addict to explain away all of them, and in this way, his denial may be overcome.

During an intervention the addict may feel like a cornered animal. After all, these people are intent on taking away from him what he feels to be the only thing that has made his life tolerable. At this point he is unable to see that their intention is to prevent his self-destruction. Rather, he feels they have somehow become evangelically inspired to make him suffer. He may not react in a kindly manner to what he considers to be an unjust assault on his personal life or may respond with vehement outrage.

It is important that everyone keep cool, and simply state what they have observed and what they plan to do if he refuses treatment. For example:

Wife: "Bill, I have always loved you and still love you. But I can no longer tolerate the behavior which your drinking/drugging is causing. If you don't accept treatment, I will have to leave you simply to protect my own sanity."

Son: "Dad, if you were only able to see what we see, you'd be the first to admit that you have a serious problem and accept treatment. I want the father I used to have. I can't relate to this other person who is the product of a chemically altered brain."

Daughter: "Daddy, you promised you would come to the play to watch me act. You didn't even remember my telling you about it. And I can't even ask my friends over to our house because I never know what you're going to be like."

Partner: "Bill, I guess I'm guilty for covering up for you when you should have been at the hospital. I can't do this any longer, nor can I take the risk of a malpractice suit if your drinking/drugging results in some mishap."

   Recovering doctor: "Bill, I know what it's like to be on the hot seat. Four years ago I was exactly where you are now and if you are as irate as I was then, you are damn angry inside. All I can tell you is that I never would have believed life could be as good as it is without alcohol/drugs."

Faced with this kind of barrage, the subject may say, "Okay, if it bothers you all that much, I'll never drink/take drugs again. You can go right over to the liquor cabinet and pour everything right down the drain. It's not worth the fuss."

At this point the intervention specialist says, "Dr. Smith, addiction is a disease, and diseases are not cured or arrested by promises. I don't doubt your good intentions, but the only way they can be implemented is by undergoing effective treatment. There are several treatment options available to you, but resolutions alone will not do the trick." Several viable treatment options should be proposed from which the subject can choose, even if it is only to which facility he will go. The coercion is traumatic enough; he should be given the opportunity to make some choice.

The subject may continue to protest vehemently that he does not need, nor will he accept treatment, so the group must stand firmly by their insistence that treatment is the only option.

It is important that no one make any threat she cannot carry out. If the wife states she cannot continue to live with an active addict, then she must be ready and able to separate. The same holds true for any of the consequences the other members of the intervention have posed. Empty threats are counterproductive.

A well-orchestrated intervention rarely fails, but it requires that the participants spend time with the intervention specialist. A dress rehearsal is most helpful. Everyone must know his own part and how to respond to the subject's reactions. A poorly conducted intervention may boomerang, with its consequences leaving nothing but bitter resentment.

People who enter treatment following an intervention may bristle with anger initially, but almost without exception this anger is dissipated and is replaced with gratitude after several days. "I never realized what was happening and what I was doing to myself. Thank God there are people around who care enough about me to save me from myself."

Implications for Treatment

Here, I would like to recapitulate the various points that have been alluded to throughout the text.

Inasmuch as the people we have discussed all suffer from the delusion that their uniqueness sets them aside from "typical" addicts, it is important that this delusion be eliminated. A proper grasp of the disease concept of addiction will do this. It is generally recognized that diabetes, pneumonia, and arthritis are not affected by a person's socioeconomic status, and when addiction is equally perceived as a disease, the uniqueness delusion will lose its strength. The problem is: How do you get the "unique" person to overcome his denial and enter treatment where he can begin to learn about the disease concept?

It is extremely helpful to initiate contact for treatment via someone with whom the client can easily identify. For example, in the Impaired Physician's Program, when we become aware of a doctor who has a chemical dependency, we have one or more recovering physicians share their experiences with him. They may take him to a physicians' AA/NA meeting, where he will meet a number of his peers and realize that his uniqueness does not preclude his being an addict. Seeing a number of recovering physicians who are enjoying active medical practice also helps allay the fear that treatment will result in exposure that will jeopardize his career.

Similar contacts can be made for lawyers, executives, educators, clergy, and others. Treatment centers can help provide contacts with other "unique" people.

It is important that family members, especially spouses, become involved in appropriate counseling and in Al-Anon or Nar-Anon family groups. Here, too, there is apt to be resistance. "What if somebody recognizes me and concludes that my husband is an alcoholic? This could ruin him." As with the chemically dependent person, there are spouses in these support groups who can be of great help to their counterparts.

There are differences of opinion about the merits of programs that treat "unique" people exclusively. It is argued that if a professional person goes to an exclusive treatment center, this only reinforces the delusion of uniqueness, and that the professional person would best be served in a center whose population is a microcosm of the community.

This objection may be overcome by the advantage of the exclusive treatment center being more acceptable to the client and therefore lowering his resistance to entering treatment. The all-important first step is to get the addicted individual into treatment. The staff of an exclusive treatment center is well-experienced in dismantling the delusion of uniqueness and if the client thinks of himself as unique when he enters, he will no longer think so when he is discharged. As a rule, people who have been treated at exclusive centers join the mainstream of recovering people in AA and NA.

It is, of course, important to get behind the façade of one's uniqueness. After attending a seminar on "The Impaired Physician," I shared this experience with a doctor who was then in treatment. His reaction to the title of the seminar was, "Impaired Physician? That's a terrible term. I am not an impaired physician at all. I am a damned good physician. I am an impaired *human being*." He was right. While there may be a unique component to a client, that is not where his addiction lies. The disease is in the person, not in his status.

As already noted, people with low self-esteem are prone to compensate for their feelings of inferiority by seeking some status of prominence. There is no need to make a frontal attack on this defense. The principles of building self-esteem should be applied so that the client can dispense with this defense himself. The self-awareness developed in the Fourth and Fifth Steps of the Twelve Step program is extremely helpful in overcoming the negative feelings the client has had for many years—often since childhood. The development of spirituality, which is the pillar of recovery, can give the person a sense of worth as a human being, totally apart from his social status or function.

All treatment programs are essentially of brief duration. Even six months of intensive treatment is "brief" for a person who enters treatment at 46, but who has been under the influence of low self-esteem for thirty-eight years and of uniqueness for perhaps twenty years. It is unrealistic to expect a total reversal after one month or even six months of treatment. What should happen is that the process of reshaping one's character and lifestyle is initiated and will continue with ongoing therapy and involvement in the recovery program.

What about "specialty" groups in the recovery programs, such as doctors', lawyers', or nurses' AA/NA groups? As noted earlier, these may serve an important function to allay the fears of an anxious newcomer that exposure of his problem will destroy him professionally or socially. Such groups can also be an important forum for sharing information about problems that confront people in these roles. However, they should not be the person's exclusive AA/NA contact. Thus, a physician or lawyer who attends a weekly or monthly AA/NA doctors' or lawyers' meeting should be attending regular meetings as well. Those who remain only with the specialty group generally do not do well in recovery.

During treatment a client should be a client and not a lawyer, doctor, financial consultant, or celebrity. In our treatment center, one client had a dislocated shoulder that an orthopedic physician then in treatment offered to treat. This was not permitted and the patient was sent to a hospital for treatment. Allowing the doctor to practice his skills while in treatment would have reinforced his uniqueness and distracted him from the focus on his addiction. Celebrities in treatment should not be allowed to give autographs. One U.S. senator requested use of an office phone to stay in touch with his senate committee business but was told that he must use the pay phone along with his fellow clients.

While frankness and self-disclosure are important, and one encourages this in group session, it is also important to respect certain aspects of privacy. This is not restricted to "unique" people. In our center, where the population is a cross-section of the community, many times a client may ask to have an individual session where he may disclose information that he feels cannot be shared with the group. This may occur with greater frequency in high-profile people, and they should be given the opportunity of privately discussing sensitive issues with a therapist. At such sessions it may turn out that this could have safely been discussed in the group, but there are also times when total privacy and confidentiality must be respected.

During treatment, a therapist should not ask a lawyer-client for legal advice or a financial planner for investment advice. These clients are usually more than happy to offer their services to staff and to fellow clients, but it should be avoided as counterproductive and antitherapeutic.

The treatment staff may have to decide when it is permissible for certain clients to assume their normal functions. A nurse-anesthetist who completed residential treatment asked for a letter approving her return to the operating room. I told her that I was incapable of assessing when it would be proper for her to return to her usual work, so I arranged a meeting with four nurses in recovery. This group concluded that early return to the O.R. was inadvisable and recommended that she not be exposed to drugs so early in her recovery. If the hospital could not find a spot for her where she did not have to handle drugs, they recommended that she take a medical leave of absence and do something else for a while. She was extremely angry with the group and had to take a job as a supermarket check-out clerk. She continued her participation in AA/NA and met with the nurses' group monthly. After one year, the group approved of her return to work and I gave her the required letter. After fifteen years of sobriety, she now admits that had she returned to the O.R. prematurely, she would likely have relapsed.

One anesthesiologist with a brilliant resumé had numerous interviews at which he was warmly received until he said, "There is something I must tell you. I am a recovering addict." The tone of the interview changed abruptly to one of: "Don't call us. We'll call you." After a year of frustration, he considered going into residency training for another specialty, since return to anesthesiology appeared hopeless. Shortly thereafter, I received a call from the department chief at one hospital where he had been interviewed, and I encouraged his being given an opportunity to return to work. He has had an excellent career there and eventually became chief of a department. He now says, "That year of unemployment was frustrating, but was just what I needed to focus on my recovery. God knew what was best for me more than I did."

Clients who are in a position where their work affects the health, safety, and welfare of others should receive monitoring for at least two years. This must be individually tailored and should include documentation of involvement in a recovery program, random urine testing, and whatever ongoing counseling is indicated. It is important to have all the legal technicalities regarding confidentiality and reporting attended to, so that the client and treatment staff understand the rules of monitoring. It is essential that the rights of the client as well as the welfare of the community be given the utmost consideration. Unique people in recovery invariably enjoy increased excellence in their performance. Many even eventually feel comfortable in disclosing the history of their addiction.

One therapist says, "I am fortunate in that my doctor, my lawyer, my dentist, my financial advisor, and my automobile mechanic are all in recovery. I have treated clients like these who had performed their functions for years while in active addiction. If my abdomen is ever to be opened, I want to be confident that the surgeon did not put away a pint of liquor the previous night and covered up his tremors with a drug prior to operating on me. The same goes for all other service providers. By having only people in recovery perform these important services for me, I can rest assured that they are functioning at their peaks."

Appendix

Professional Groups and Organizations Dealing with Alcoholism and Drug Dependency

A. Limited to alcoholic or chemically dependent people.

   1. *Attorneys*
      International Lawyers in A.A. (ILAA)
      111 Pearl Street, Room 202
      Hartford, Connecticut 06103
      (203) 527-1854

      English Alcoholic Group for Lawyers (EAGL)
      A. Robinson, M.A., Co-Ordinator
      Morrab Villa, PENZANCE
      Cornwall TR18 4DQ, U.K.
      0736.68369
        or
      English Alcoholic Group for Lawyers (EAGL)
      John Eccles
      1 Stoneham House
      13 Queens Road
      Richmond, Surrey TW10 6JW
      01.940.9163

   2. *Clergy* (Anglican)
      Recovered Alcoholic Clergy Assn. (RACA)
      647 Dundee Avenue
      Barrington, Illinois 60010
      (312) 381-2323

3. *Psychologists*
Psychologists Helping Psychologists
Jane Skorina, Ph.D.
23439 Michigan Street
Dearborn, Michigan 48124
(313) 565-3821

B. Limited to those who have had a personal (rather than professional) experience with alcoholism or other chemical dependency. Includes Al-Anon members.

1. *Physicians, dentists, and other doctoral-level, health-care professionals*
International Doctors in A.A.
1950 Volney Road
Youngstown, Ohio 44511
(216) 782-6216

2. *Nurses*—See NNSA (E-2, below)

3. *Social Workers*
Social Workers Helping Social Workers
Contact:
John F. Fitzgerald, M.S.W., Ph.D.
Route #63
Goshen, Connecticut 06756
(203) 491-2490 or (203) 566-2696

C. Composed largely of persons having had personal experience with alcoholism or chemical dependency but members include others.

1. *Attorneys*
Lawyers Concerned for Lawyers
610 Chamber of Commerce Bldg.
15 5th Street South
Minneapolis, Minnesota 55402
(612) 339-1230

2. *Anthropologists*
Anthropologists Concerned for Anthropologists
c/o James M. Schaefer, Ph.D.
Office of Alcohol and Other Drug Abuse Programming
Room 360
2610 University Avenue
St. Paul, Minnesota 55114

3. *Clergy (Catholic)*
National Clergy Council on Alcoholism and Related Drug
   Problems
3112 7th Street N.E.
Washington, D.C. 20017
(202) 832-3811

4. *Nuns (Catholic)*
ICAP
2510 N. Drake
Chicago, Illinois 60647
(312) 342-1413

5. *Dentists*
Dentists Concerned for Dentists
610 Chamber of Commerce Bldg.
15 5th Street South
Minneapolis, Minnesota 55402
(612) 339-1068

6. *Physicians*
Physicians Serving Physicians
610 Chamber of Commerce Bldg.
15 5th Street South
Minneapolis, Minnesota 55402
(612) 339-0711

British Doctor's Group
c/o The Medical Council on Alcoholism
3 Grosvenor Crescent, London SWIX, U.K.
01-235-4182
(*Correspondence can be marked "Please forward unopened" if desired.*)

7. *Gay/lesbian* (*multidisciplinary*)
National Association of Gay Alcoholism Professionals
Dana Finnigan, Ph.D.
204 W. 20th Street
New York, New York 10011
(212) 807-0634

The organizations listed above (sections A, B, and C) are primarily advocacy and support groups and will not attempt to coerce, discipline, or police those who seek their help. There are many state-level groups and committees. Some are limited to offering help, keep no records, make no reports to other agencies, and avoid any attempt to manage or monitor. Others are frankly disciplinary and operate more as extensions of licensing boards. Still others have combined functions. All 50 state medical societies now have impaired physician committees.

D. State associations and professional organizations *not* primarily composed of recovered individuals.

1. *Catholic Nuns* (*includes nursing orders*)
Sister Maurice Doody
Office of New Directions
2341 University Avenue
Bronx, New York 10468
(212) 365-5730

2. *Dentists*
   Council on Dental Practice
   American Dental Association
   211 East Chicago Avenue
   Chicago, Illinois 60611
   (800) 621-8099
   Contact: H. Kendal Beachman, Secretary
           or
   Dr. John C. Clarno
   Special Consultant
   ADA Alcohol/Drug Program
   Parkside Medical
   1580 N. Northwest Highway
   Park Ridge, Illinois 60068
   (312) 696-8200

3. *Pharmacists*
   Richard P. Penna, Pharm.D.
   American Pharmaceutical Assn.
   2215 Constitution Avenue, N.W.
   Washington, D.C. 20037
   (202) 628-4410

4. *Physicians*
   Health and Human Behavior Program
   AMA
   535 North Dearborn Street
   Chicago, Illinois 60610
   (312) 751-6000
   (Maintains list of impaired physician committees.)

George Esselman, D.O.
Texas College of Osteopathic Medicine
Camp Bowie at Montgomery Street
Ft. Worth, Texas 76107
(817) 735-2561
(Has information about state committees within osteopathic medicine.)

5. *Nurses*
   Several states, including Ohio and Maryland, now have impaired nurse committees and will share information through their state nursing associations.

E. Professional organizations that focus on alcoholism and chemical dependence whose memberships are limited to specific disciplines and who have available information on specific committees within their ranks for helping impaired colleagues.

1. *Clergy (interfaith)*
   North Conway Institute
   14 Beacon Street
   Boston, Massachusetts 02108

2. *Nurses*
   Drug and Alcohol Nursing Assn., Inc. (DANA)
   Box 371
   College Park, Maryland 20740

   National Nurses Society on Addictions (NNSA)
   2506 Gross Point Road
   Evanston, Illinois 60201

One professional working in Kansas is assembling a directory of A.A. and other support groups for nurses and is already able to direct callers to many groups and individuals:

Pat Green, R.N.
1020 Sunset Drive
Lawrence, Kansas 66044
(913) 842-3893

3. *Physicians*
American Medical Society on Alcoholism
12 West 21 Street
New York, New York 10010
(212) 206-6770

There are over 40 local groups for medical professionals which are similar to, but independent of, IDAA. Many other groups for special populations exist, such as:

JACS Foundation
c/o New York Board of Rabbis
10 East 73rd Street
New York, New York 10021
(212) 737-6261

which provides networking and support services to Jewish alcoholics and has a large number of professionals in its membership.

General

Many of these groups are known to the General Service Office of Alcoholics Anonymous, Box 459, Grand Central Station, New York, New York 10163, and, while not listed in official A.A. directories, are on file. Although interested in the more broad promotion of physical and mental well-being rather than in alcoholism per se and primarily for health-care professionals, additional information and materials can be obtained from:

Center for Professional Well-Being
5102 Chapel Hill Blvd.
Durham, North Carolina 27707
(919) 489-9167

In 1983 an association of employee assistance programs that provides services to hospitals was formed. It plans to share information, develop standards, and provide general support. Contact through:

Association of Labor-Management Administrators and
    Consultants on Alcoholism (ALMACA)
1800 North Kent Street
Suite 907
Arlington, Virginia 22209
(703) 522-6272

Suggestions for Further Reading

Ackerman, R. (1993). *Silent Sons*. New York: Simon & Schuster.

Beattie, M. (1992). *CoDependent No More*. Center City, MN: Hazelden.

Bissel, L., and Haberman, P. W. (1984). *Alcoholism in the Professions*. New York: Oxford Univesity Press.

Bradshaw, J. (1988). *Healing the Shame That Binds You*. Deerfield Beach, FL: Health Communications.

Daley, D. (1988). *Surviving Addiction*. New York: Gardner.

Duffy, J. C., and Litin, E. M. (1967). *The Emotional Health of Physicians*. Springfield, IL: Charles C Thomas.

Earle, M. (1989). *Physician Heal Thyself*. Minneapolis, MN: CompCare.

Hansen, P. (1982). *Alcoholism: The Tragedy of Abundance*. Minneapolis, MN: Park Printing.

Hollis, J. (1985). *Fat Is a Family Affair*. Center City, MN: Hazelden.

Johnson, V. E. (1980). *I'll Quit Tomorrow*. New York: Harper & Row.

——— (1996). *Intervention: How to Help Someone Who Doesn't Want to Be Helped*. Minneapolis, MN: Johnson Institute.

Liebelt, R. A. (1989). *Straight Talk About Alcoholism*. New York: Paros.

Robe, L. B. (1986). *Famous Women and Alcoholism*. Minneapolis, MN: CompCare.

Schuckit, M. A. (1995). *Drug and Alcohol Abuse*. New York: Plenum.

Staubman, S. (1994). *Ending the Struggle Against Yourself*. New York: Putnam.

Twerski, A. (1997). *Addictive Thinking*. Center City, MN: Hazelden.

——— (1995). *Life's Too Short*. New York: Henry Holt.

——— (1996). *I'd Like to Call for Help, but I Don't Know the Number*. New York: Henry Holt.

Index

**LINEBERGER
MEMORIAL LIBRARY
LUTHERAN THEOLOGICAL
SOUTHERN SEMINARY**
COLUMBIA, SOUTH CAROLINA 29203

DEMCO